SKI-WISE

John Samuel

London
GEORGE ALLEN & UNWIN
Boston   Sydney

First published in 1977

© George Allen & Unwin (Publishers) Ltd, 1977

ISBN 0 04 796048 5

Printed in Great Britain
in 11 on 12 point Baskerville
at the Alden Press, Oxford.

Contents

Illustrations

Acknowledgements

Ski-ing, as well as being the riskiest sport I have tried, is also the most generous. It so often brings out the best characteristics in people – a willingness to share and communicate not least. I am indebted to many in the preparation of this book, all of whom have in common their enthusiasm for ski-ing, and the wish that others will come to like it similarly. My especial thanks to Jane Fawkes, of the Ski Club of Great Britain, who encouraged me to think I had something to communicate; to Douglas Godlington, of the British Association of Ski Instructors Committee, who has provided descriptive drawings with a careful regard to beginners; to photographer friends and fellow ski enthusiasts, Stewart Fraser and Don Morley; to Ian Graeme, secretary, and John Shedden, director of coaching, at the National Ski Federation, for guidance, goodwill and use of material; to Mike Browne, of Alpine Sports, who has contributed diagrams, Michael Evans of Pindisports, Martin Grace of Lillywhites, and Sandy Caird of Cairdsport for their advice on equipment and clothes; to Dr John Williams of Farnham Park Rehabilitation Centre, Secretary of the International Sports Medicine Federation, for his skill in patching me up after a ski accident, and for permission to use the Centre's fitness schedule to the advantage of anyone intending a ski holiday; to Angela Jones of Inghams Travel for her patience with my many queries; to Oliver Hart of Salomon for advice on one of the most critical aspects of ski-ing, bindings and their release properties; to Barbara Bush of *Ski Magazine*, USA, for information on technique, and especially the US learning system, GLM; to Anthony Churchill, of *Ski Magazine*, Britain, for permission to use the best available resort guide, list of ski shops and other records; to tourist officers in London, among them Knut Søvorr (Norway), Norbert Burda (Austria), Jurge Schmid (Switzerland), and Pauline Hallam (France); to Guy Chilver-Stainer, secretary-treasurer of the Scottish National Ski Council, and H. A. McKellar, head of the Glasgow Weather Centre, for their help with Scottish ski-ing; to Major-General Reginald Leathes, who knows so much of ski-ing, for advising on the text; and finally to the *Guardian* for making so many of my ski journeys possible.

Introduction

This is a book mostly for people who want to ski and have never done so. It is also for those who tried it ten to twenty years ago, and with family or other commitments off their hands want advice and encouragement about starting again. It is for people who are city dwellers, or live hundreds of miles from regular snow, but yearn for the pure air and wide vistas of high places. Ski-ing, more than any sport I know, lifts and renews the spirit. It needs no other justification.

My qualifications for attempting the task are mixed. Mainly I have gone out to the mountains to write about racing ski-ing. Sometimes that involves a lengthy, foot-stamping wait at the bottom of the mountain, a few glances at the hooded TV in the finish enclosure, some chat with the racers, and a sharp dart back to the type-writer. To me that is cheating – cheating myself. I also like to ski. The racer is the Formula One man (or woman) capable of three and four times my speed, but my exhilaration in a pair of silvery traces over the broad, high alm or through the fir and spruce avenues is little different because my speed is that much slower. The racer gives much to ski-ing – excitement and colour to the armchair follower; new ideas on how to ski; the impetus for technical change which has revolutionised all ski-ing in the past ten years. But enjoyment? That is for us all – and if a dash of his danger rubs off, then we can cope with that too!

It is three years since I began writing this book, but the changes were happening so fast that I had continuously to stop and reconsider the evidence, to decide what was modish – and no sport is more vulnerable to fashion and mere gimmickry – and what might be enduring. It does seem now that there is a kind of plateau. The major enduring advances in the sport during the last few years have been:

1. The establishment of a stable short ski, thanks to modern manufacturing methods, as a better means of getting novices started. It makes learning easier and helps the intermediate to advanced skier able to spare only a fortnight a year for the sport.

2. The adaptation of learning techniques to a shorter ski, best exemplified in the twin US and Continental systems, GLM and Ski Evolutif.

3. Bootmaking, which has looked more scientifically at the need to lock sideways ankle movement, and to transfer essential heel-and-toe and knee-and-thigh pressures to the skis and their edges.

4. Bindings (the means by which boots are secured to skis) with safer release properties.

5. Groomed slopes, especially in the USA and France, which have encouraged better learning methods.

6. Purpose-built resorts at altitudes where snow is more reliable, which offer a genuine alternative to the village-

turned-resort. I am not saying that one should be preferred to the other, only that the choice should exist.

7. Self-catering as a cheaper alternative to hotel or guest-house living.

8. The much increased sophistication and scope of the Scottish scene, which gives ski-ing a genuine home base.

9. For Britons generally, the establishment of more than seventy artificial slopes which introduce youngsters, especially, to the activity at an age when they can most readily learn.

10. A British retail trade of increasing knowledge in the provision of up-to-date clothes and equipment.

11. The increasing attraction of different ski forms: freestyle, cross-country and grass.

12. Operator and club services which are constantly seeking cheaper answers to inflationary pressures.

This is not a technical manual. I want to guide the novice or relative novice from his home to the snow, setting out the choices with the most important and up-to-date information at my disposal. If at the same time I can interest more experienced skiers I shall be happy. Sooner or later in ski-ing, everyone has to face the fall line, the moment the skis point directly down the steepest part of the mountain. At that point no book will help. But much can be done to prepare for the moment, to enjoy things in prospect, and then to build quickly on hard-won confidence.

Chapter I

Ski-wise

The first thing any skier has to do is to get up the hill in order to come down. Between desire and accomplishment lies a range of uphill transport devices – the soup plate or button lift, the evil-looking, pickaxe T-bar, the open chair, the cable and bubble cars, the funicular. At Val d'Isère one year they were mighty short both of snow and of enough lift capacity to take racing teams and officials to the Col de l'Iseran, hard by the glacier, where the World Cup races had been transferred. Waiting for the soup plate I found myself sandwiched between two Olympic champions, the Austrian world champion, Karl Schranz, and another senior team member. A barrier to the rear prevented queue jumping, but it also served to block escape. The tow would not normally have presented problems, but it was adjusted for another metre of snow. The springs were tough and rusted, with little give. The act of placing the circle of plastic between the legs was best accompanied by a prayer, for the lift-off flung the rider a good metre into the air. This was the first major race of the season, and Schranz's English was good enough, and my German bad enough, to convey an adequate message that he needed the snow-time more than me. Would he take my place ahead? He thanked me politely, flitted from my left to my right on one poised ski stick, then broke every tow law by dumping himself so heavily on the plastic plate it all but touched the ground. The spring contracted violently, he flew not one metre but two in his team-mate's wake, and was gone like Mary Poppins.

Ski-ing has rules rather than laws and, while some can be broken or bent, others may not. Schranz could bend more laws than most because his experience and fitness enabled him to pick out the patterns vastly quicker than Jenny, a 23-year-old London secretary on her first ski-ing trip. For the purpose of this book I am going to adopt Jenny and her casual boy-friend, Michael. They are both going on a ski-ing holiday for the first time, in a group of five. Jenny is keen to learn and a bit of a sticker. She has heard that ski-ing is a hard as well as a glamorous sport – she was almost put off completely when someone told her that there was a pain barrier to cross before she could hope to enjoy it fully. Jenny's weakness is that she cannot resist a bit of a challenge. We shall leave her from time to time, but ski-ing is like that: people tend to pop in or pop up then disappear, if only temporarily.

Ski-ing since the war has been a major growth sport. Its origins are recent; 1936 was the first year that Alpine, or downhill, ski racing took place in a Winter Olympic Games. Until then the Nordic countries, Norway, Sweden and Finland, had contemptuously dismissed the gimmicky notion of ski-ing downhill. Partly this was because their own mountains are lower, with much more gentle slopes than the Alps. Partly it is because the average Norwegian has a snowcraft based on the need to travel and communicate, not just to play. The Scandinavians ski uphill as much as down, and this is the essential difference between Nordic, or cross-country, ski-ing and Alpine, where you only climb if you overshoot the lift take-off, and then with a curse. The hard work is due to the difference in equipment. A few years ago, Jenny would never have set eyes on a Nordic skier in the Alps, seen their looping graceful strides; wooden skis, slim and graceful as a stork's beak, and parkas over breeches and knee stockings. Now they are likely to be anywhere on Alpine foothills, paths and frozen lakes, the chief difference being that the skis are mostly of glass fibre.

It is hard to be sure of exactly how many people ski. Britain's statistic of half a million is more accurate than some because 300,000 pass through tour operators en route to the Continent of Europe, but while the number of English booking for Scotland is easy to assess (it is still only a small proportion of those going to Europe), it is harder to judge just how many skiers there are from Edinburgh, Glasgow, Aberdeen and other big Scottish ski areas. Cairngorm, on a good Saturday, will have 2,000 cars overspilling its parks. Downtown Montreal is almost deserted on a fine week-end, while the cars stream up the autoroute to the Laurentians or down to the eastern townships. Mount Whistler, above Vancouver, can absorb at least 6,000 people, mostly from the one city, and the villages above Innsbruck, Grenoble and Milan three and four times as many. One estimate puts it at ten million skiers in Europe and six million in the USA, though the growth of Nordic ski-ing, especially in North America, is making nonsense of this. Mount Orford, a popular mountain just over the US border in Quebec Province, had 18,000 Nordic skiers on its various trails in 1974, but 25,000 by February 1975. Four years before there had been none.

In 1975, too, the short-ski revolution really took hold. 'The shortening of America', the US magazine, *Ski*, described it, and the rest of the ski world had to sit up and take notice of more unwritten rules broken and a new

vogue setting in. Just as important was the revolution in
boot design which made comfort and edge control
available together for the first time. Such was the competition that prices remained amazingly stable. Mean-
while freestyle ski-ing both fed and was serviced by the
shorter ski revolution, and aerials (acrobatics) and ballet
joined with bumps ski-ing in another new wave. 'My
flight plan at Snowbird (a Rocky Mountain resort not far
from Salt Lake City) is a front flyaway tuck, a back
layout and a triple daffy,' one freestyler pro announced,
and there were people to understand her. Scotland
quickly picked up the styles and the jargon, but the rest
of Europe has stayed a little more po-faced; tradition
dies hard in the Arlberg and the Bernese Oberland. But
in France, particularly, there has been a revolution in
self-catering which has much reduced costs, and the
ingenuity of tour operators has continually defied the
worst red tape of the International Air Transporters'
Association. Ski-ing will never be a cheap sport, but there
are more and less expensive ways of doing things, as there
are better and quicker ways of learning. Why on earth,
though, do we do it at all? If I first offer my own early
experiences it is in the hope that others may find an
echo in them, and that those who have still to try the
sport will have some idea of its challenges and enjoy-
ments – as well as some clue to the short cuts now
available.

In some ways it was a simpler world when I began in
1954, partly because the choices were much narrower,
but many of the lessons I learnt stay valid today. Things
had moved on since 1903, when Sir Arnold Lunn's father
gave him a Christmas present of a pair of skis costing
twenty Swiss francs, and a pair of boots worth thirty

francs, the equivalent of £2. Sir Arnold, subsequently the founder of the Kandahar racing club in Mürren, Switzerland, and inventor of the slalom ski race, quickly discovered as a boy that his equipment to some extent dictated his technique. It still does. 'On my first pair of ski,' Sir Arnold recounted, 'I could not turn abruptly without my foot coming right off the ski. I reduced speed by leaning heavily on a single pole. I zig-zagged across steeper slopes and kick-turned to change direction. On the gentler slopes I stopped by dragging myself round my single pole. I skied for three winters before I saw a skier execute S-turns down a slope.'

In 1954, fifty years later, the package tour boom was still to mushroom, and the group which mustered, nervously and a little in awe, at the Ski Club of Great Britain's premises in Eaton Square, London, was there under the auspices of the Central Council of Physical Recreation. This was not so much a holiday as an expedition. We were there to learn rather than to enjoy ourselves. Fitness training for the London-based was at Chelsea Barracks, but when the party of fifty finally gathered at Newcastle there were as many from the North as from the South of England. We were paying about £50 for our fortnight at Geilo, Norway's no. 2 ski resort, a quiet, unpretentious place of about one thousand souls on the Bergen–Oslo railway line. In my first enthusiasm I had run to a pair of ski boots, bought from a sports shop for £6 in a closing-down sale. The first seeds of failure were in those boots. Even in Norway, not notably a radical country, they were scrutinised carefully and closely, and politely set down as antiques. They were leather, it is true, as were all respectable ski boots of that time, but moulded with an eye to economy rather than efficiency: the leather, giving out halfway up the ankle bone, was just enough to bruise, yet not enough to support.

Perhaps we did not think ourselves socially prepared for the Alps, for ski-ing then still held assumptions of money and class which a young sub-editor with Reuters on £750 a year was unsure about. We lined up at Geilo in khaki unisex hand-me-downs. It was early January and low season in Norway, which at best can mean a sun blearily lolling over the southern horizon like a melon too long on the stall. Arnie Palm, a former Norwegian international skier, whose ski school at Geilo is still renowned, quickly assigned what appeared to be the more athletic group to an instructor I will call Stig. Stig was a brave man, having paddled a small boat across the North Sea to England during the war to join the Royal Air Force. He was a barrister from Oslo who instructed for pleasure, so we were told. The threat he held over the men for the remaining ten days was that we would be banished to join the women if we did not come up to scratch. As we were 1950s men not long out of National Service, and from single-sex schools where to be dropped from the first team was a fate little short of death, this was a potent threat.

Our issue skis were wooden, 200 centimetres long, with variable Kandahar bindings. The wire of the binding could be reset on the lugs of the ski so that we could lift our heels two to three inches for touring ski-ing. The wire needed to be tightened, clamping our heels firmly to the skis, for downhill ski-ing, which in effect was when a slope exceeded about fifteen degrees. There may have been a nursery slope tow, but Stig ignored it. Norway's puritanism, I believe, is skin deep, the closed bars from Friday night to Monday merely the other side of the desire to drink to the dregs. Stig had me wondering. What goes up must come down was an aphorism he reversed. If we went down fifty yards in a series of linked plough turns, he made sure we climbed all the way up again.

The plough is the 'V' position, with the tips of the skis close together but not quite touching and the tails splayed out behind, by which the skier first gets down the hill under some sort of control. If you put more of your weight on your right-hand ski you will turn left, and if more on the left you will turn right. It is rather like learning to row, with the boat turning the opposite way to the one you expect. It takes time for the message to sift through the reluctant brain into the subconscious, where a great deal in ski-ing ultimately belongs. Ploughing is also known as stemming. Stig's benevolent tyranny ensured a plough turn cast in concrete; fifteen years later, with ski instruction styles much changed and the plough turn important, but much more a transitional phase, I was still trying to chip away the last of the concrete. In ski-ing you come to be aware that the right piece of advice at the right time can make a great deal of difference. It can be only one thing, for the mind cannot hold on to more. Early learning requires a flexibility. I did not properly understand why a ski is shaped as it is, what its various properties are, and I did not relate them to my plough turn. That was earliest and most enduring hang-up.

These were the days of wooden skis, and hire skis, like hire cars, suffer a great deal of use in a limited time. Wooden skis had to be taken care of; they were best stood on their tips to preserve the shovel curve; they had to be blocked up every spring so that their camber, or arch, was preserved while they were laid up; they had to be waxed regularly and for differing conditions; and their metal edges had to be carefully checked for screws pulling out. Today's skis, making wide use of man-made materials and metal, do not require such attention – and probably do not command such love. My skis at Geilo felt like boards, with none of the springiness I have since learned to seek, and in so far as I considered them at all my view was neutral.

Stig, to give him his due, tried to drive us on to the stem christie, where one ski is lifted or slid to the side of the other during the course of the turn. He did his damnedest, lifting and lowering himself in that exaggerated movement universally thought necessary in those days to demonstrate weighting and unweighting, though how that was going to get my skis to turn quietly baffled me. On a rather steeper slope reserved for stem christie solos, I waited my turn with cotton wool filling my skull. I was fairly athletic, still playing soccer and cricket regularly, and as my turn approached I resolved that my performance would at least show a level of fitness. I pushed off under Stig's hard eye, my mind firmly in control. But as the ground slid away under me the unequal battle once again was lost, the body and all its inadequate responses leading the mind panic-stricken in its wake. With one last major effort before gravity took total control, I yelled at myself, 'Jump!' Stig in his demonstration had in fact appeared to leap, though this was a trifle misleading, and anyway his skis had followed him. I leapt, body twisting and rising, but only from the knees. Boots and feet stayed much where they were, the skis with them, doing about fifteen mph. The effect, in one frozen moment, must have been extraordinary – rather like those leaping, snarling animals on Jaguar car bonnets. Muscles and ligaments grated and wrenched, and I fell over in a series of loose cartwheels. Stig came and quietly handed back my ski sticks and other bits. For a moment it was in his eye and on his tongue to tell me quietly to go and join the others – the girls. But there was only a day left, and he turned and skated off, while I very slowly clipped the wires back under the lugs and returned to my chains, to my capable ploughing. No more was said.

The following year I tried Seefeld, Austria, an established resort under an hour's train ride north of Innsbruck, altitude 3872 feet, twenty-two hotels and seventeen inns and pensions, and a reputation for liveliness rather than expert ski-ing. Seefeld sits on a sunny shelf, with terrain immediately around the village suitable for cross-country ski-ing, and indeed the Mieminger Plateau was the Nordic centre for the Innsbruck Winter Olympic Games of 1964 and 1976. It had – still has – a jolly, holiday camp feel to it, and three of us making up a party from our original CCPR venture perhaps succumbed unduly to the easy, sybarite atmosphere, with beer on draught flowing freely, plenty of oompah dancing at night, and an exchange rate of seventy-two schillings to the pound. Austria was at this time the only country seriously encouraging the package tour, and F. and W. Ingham had provided train, room and board at an ancient, booming inn for £50 or thereabouts. The Gschwandt-kopf, close by our pub, offered relatively easy ski-ing for second-year people, but the Seefelder Joch, on the other side of the village, at 6000 feet, offered a different story. I had been too mean to throw away my 'antique' boots after only ten days' wear and now I really regretted it. The first day at ski school brought up the ankle bruises again, our hotel was a good ten minutes walk from the nursery slopes, and once more I was in agony.

On this holiday I probably made every mistake there is to make on a ski holiday. I stayed up too late. My anorak, a bargain I had thought, was too thin when the weather turned rough. My hire skis were poor, with ragged edges, and I was either too diffident or too preoccupied to replace them. After a particularly late night the ski school instructor decided this was the day to take us to the top of the Seefelder Joch. It had snowed a bit in the village, but even he was surprised by the metre which lay thick and heavy at the top. The descent was utter misery. Within the first few yards, I fell. Happily the binding, still the cable type, released in spite of the slowness of the fall, but to clean off the sole of my boot in thigh deep snow was beyond me. Consequently a quarter-inch layer of snow lay between my boot and the ski, weakening the grip of my binding and affecting control of the ski. My tenuous grasp of soft-snow ski-ing technique had not been helped by Austrian teaching, which was going through agonies of change. That year, counter-rotation had become all the rage. Whatever the direction of the skis, the skier was supposed to point his chest and shoulders downhill, and the number of slipped discs among Austrian ski instructors reached epidemic proportions. Slipping, sliding, falling down the last stages of the Rosshütte run, I was in a state of mental and physical exhaustion where the words counter-rotation would have made as much sense in medieval High German.

I was left with a few elementary lessons: never to ski with a hangover; the importance of comfortable but supportive boots and a lined anorak; the necessity to clean all the snow off my boot soles before stepping into the ski bindings; and preferably a hotel close to ski school and/or lifts. I was struck by the value of package tours, though making a mental note to add about two-thirds of the price to the original quotation to allow for lift tickets, drinks and extras; and I learned something of the meaning of gemütlichkeit in the cheaper bars where local people gathered, and at the local farmers' dance in the town hall where the girls dressed like Tyrolean dolls and never said no to a dance. It was not a great deal, perhaps, but enough of a ski-ing experience to keep the pilot light aflame over the next eight years of marriage and a young family. Then came the chance, through my work on the

sports department of the *Guardian*, to renew my interest
in winter sport and especially in ski-ing.

There are many men and even more women who find
themselves starting to ski again in their middle thirties.
Quite a few at that age are trying it for the first time.
Nearly always the gap or the late start is due to family
pressures – the children are too young to be taken, the
family too close-budgeted for summer and winter holidays.
But a ski trip lingers in the back of the mind as something
all the family can enjoy when the children are old
enough. If the money does not run to it for all the family
at once, then perhaps it will be a school trip for the
children, and later on an older family party with the
children able to pay for themselves. Continental families,
with the Alps closer at hand, are better placed than the
British or the many US families who are eight to twelve
hours by car away from East Coast or Rocky Mountain
ski centres. Anyway, when Jenny attends her first ski
school, she will not lack mature company in those first
awkward attempts to ski, and the more people around
with a knowledge of life's figurative ups and downs, the
easier and funnier it will be to cope with the actual.

Nine years after I took off my skis at Seefeld I was
clipping myself into a pair of Attenhofer skis on the top
of the nursery slope at Grindelwald. Step-in bindings were
still the exception rather than the rule at Swiss hire shops,
and once again I found myself trying to force the clip of
the Kandahar binding forward on one foot, while the
other ski slid from under me on the other. I collapsed in a
rather painful heap, only this time I had the audience of
a wife to hoot with laughter. To a backdrop of the
Wetterhorn and Eiger mountains, I kept telling myself,
'It's just like cycling. You never forget.' Up to a point
this is true. All ski-ing time is knowledge in the bank. But
the deposits are more accessible after one year's lapse than

nine, and the knowledge stored was of questionable value.

The outdoor swimming pool at Alpe d'Huez, France, looked invitingly blue under the noon sun. It was still only February, but the Savoie resorts in the south-west Alps can seem touched by the Mediterranean. Outdoor swimming amid banks of snow is, after all, a bit exotic. After the initial plunge the water felt agreeably warm. The pool was about thirty-five metres and, a reasonably strong swimmer, I struck out with a confident crawl for the far end. At twenty metres the crawl dissolved into a panting, near-static dog paddle. I had failed completely to allow for the effects of an altitude of 6,000 feet.

Swimming is a particularly strenuous sport – if the average man's resting heart rate is seventy-two, the racing swimmer's is likely to be forty. In other words, he has to oxygenate his system with less effort than the ordinary man. Some people, quite naturally, make their lungs work more efficiently than others, literally using more of the balloon. The sudden explosive grunt of the karate performer is not an expression of feeling. He is expelling stale air from the bottom of his lungs. Jenny, dodging up the Underground escalators from time to time, walking the three hundred yards to and from her flat, does not get anywhere near the regular exercise of the racing swimmer. All these things will begin to have a bearing when she stoops to tighten the clips on her ski boots outside the lift. She is at 6,000 feet, and the air will be thinner, or less oxygenated. Her heart will have to work harder to achieve even a simple objective like bending down to do up clips. Fatigue will come sooner than she expects; in fact it will overtake her before she is aware. Ski-ing is a risk sport, but the risks which are less easily calculated are the most dangerous. Like the man unaware that he has drunk a little too much, the tired skier loses objective judgement about his own condition and becomes a danger to himself and others.

I know a girl, no older than Jenny, who can get out of the Solaise cable car at Val d'Isère, put on her skis, and ski the huge mogul field, moulded like a monster golf ball, up and down all day. Her technique is so good, her attitude so relaxed, that she barely breaks into a sweat. Gravity does most of the work for her. The fact that she wears contact lenses is neither here nor there. She is planning her route through and over the bumps with quick, certain appreciations, and with a relaxation that gives her seemingly endless stamina. She has been a travel operator's representative for several seasons, and no-one can become a truly first-class skier in all conditions without three or four solid months in a mountain environment.

Most nursery slopes, for beginners of all ages, are close to village centres, and traditional Alpine villages tend to be at lowish levels (they were built for sphepherds and foresters, not skiers). In both the Alps and the Rockies, though, purpose-built ski resorts are being established at higher levels, where the snow is more reliable, and even beginners on slopes right next to their hotels must make allowance for the effects of altitude on themselves. The simple business of climbing the stairs to your room will take a much bigger physical toll. Suddenly you feel dizzy and slightly sick, perhaps a little panicky, wondering what is happening to you. The sensations, known more precisely as vertigo, are common enough. Jenny once suffered it blowing up a lilo on a beach. Most sportsmen get it at one time or the other but skiers more than most. It is to do with excitement and altitude. Even at sea level, as she sat puffing at the lilo spout on the beach, Jenny was hyper-ventilating, or over-breathing, much as a skier might. She began to feel sick and dizzy, but the moment she stopped blowing the sensations passed. Similarly, the skier at altitude is breathing much more deeply than normally, there is a build-up of excitement and tension, and there is little for the moment that he or she can do about it. Carbon dioxide, or stale air, is being forced out of the lungs where it has perhaps been little disturbed for some time. The effect has sometimes rendered people unconscious. If the lilo sensation overtakes Jenny at the top of the run through the build-up of tension and adrenalin she has to stop, allow her breathing to relax, look round – and make the others wait. Their turn to be affected is likely to come soon enough, whether they fall, miss the way or suddenly grow tired.

Excitement and apprehension are shared in some degree by every skier. Once, travelling in the Chantarella funicular railway at St Moritz, John Hennessey, sports editor and ski racing correspondent of *The Times*, looked lugubriously round him, at young men dressed like ski-ing Uhlans, at trim girls, their eyes concealed mysteriously behind large smoked glasses, and murmured: 'Do you ever get the feeling in a situation like this that you must be the worst skier in the whole of the cabin?' The answer was, of course, yes. The fact that a third of the people on the train were only up there to develop a tan was soon apparent enough. Skiers have a constant battle with the ego. Over-awareness and over-concern will lead to a chicken state of mind where troubles will be compounded, not eased. Tony Jacklin once said about golf that if you stand on the tee and look long enough at a single tree on the fairway it will become not a tree but a forest. There is a type of mental blocking out which is healthy and a type which is not, and Jenny, I hope, will come to sort it out with a few practical drills. But it is no good pretending in the funicular or cabin car that the movement and height are not worrying when they are. It is a natural enough reaction which will be further compounded when you first begin to slide on your skis. The first movement on skis, the first loss of familar orientation as the hill begins to slide past at increasing speed, is a moment of sheer panic for most adults. Children, being closer to the ground, and in any case more flexibly muscled and boned, may worry less – but not necessarily.

It is all to do with the eyes and the middle ear. One simple illustration is the sensation which most people will have felt of slight sickness when travelling in a train with their backs to the engine. Their eyes are not accustomed to things flashing by in the opposite direction, and vertigo sets in. The same thing may happen on a cable car several hundred feet off the ground, especially if it is rising above broken ground, precipitous in places, which imposes further focal strains on the eye. Simply to know that this is taking place and that the eye is in process of adjustment often eases the sensation of dizziness or sickness. The best alternative is to focus on something constant, on the person you are with in the car, or even on the ceiling. If the big wheel at the funfair is causing problems at the top or on the downswing, then you tell your children to stare at the sky. The principle is the same. Once the skier is clipped into his skis, the eye has a much more positive, linked role with muscle, bone and ligament, and to help it out in the act of balancing there are two other important organs.

Floating in the Alpe d'Huez pool with eyes closed I could still point perfectly accurately to my left foot, or know whether my right leg was bent, without any sighting aids. This is because of the vestibular apparatus, situated on either side of the head just next to the ear and made up of two clever but simple organs. The first is a jelly-like structure called the utricle, containing many fine nerve hairs. If the head is bent to one side the weight of the jelly makes the hairs fall to that side, passing the information to the brain. If a skier leans to one side to absorb a bump, the message is quickly relayed and the brain at once leans the body the other way to maintain balance. The second organ is made up of three small circular tubes, linked rather like a clover leaf, but at right angles to each other, and filled with fluid. One lies on each of the planes of movement, like three adjacent sides of a box. The fluid inside each canal adopts a position according to the place of the head in that plane. The three together exactly define the position of the head. These organs send their key messages to the brain, which, with its 1,000,000,000 nerve cells, programmes a physical response. The worst skier in the cabin is a cleverer scientific vehicle than Apollo 16. It is a comforting thought for the beginner and one reason, perhaps, why he needs to challenge something as beautiful and dangerous as a mountain.

Chapter 2

Where Shall We Go?

At one time you did not choose a resort as much as it chose you. The house rules from the historic Christiana Inn, Whistler Mountain, Alta Lake, British Columbia, are as follows:

> You must pay you rent in advance.
> You must not let you room go back one day.
> Women is not allow in you room.
> If you wet or burn you bed you going out.
> You are not allow to gambel in you room.
> You are not allow to give you bed to you freand.
> If you freand stay overnight you must see the manager.
> You must leave you room at 12 am so the women can clean you room.
> Only on Sunday you can sleep all day.
> You are not allow in the seating room or in the dinering room when you are drunk.
> You are not allow to drink on the front porch.
> You must use a shirt when you come to the seating room.
> If you cant keep this rules please dont take the room.

Well, you knew where you stood in 1901. Compare that with Val d'Isère's little poem to itself:

> Val d'Isere, yesterday, Val, forever, Val.
> Reigning for over a thousand years from the
>   depths of her valley,
> Alert and tenacious as an eagle on its eyrie.
> Courageous Val, predominating the
>   mountains, from age to age, slope to slope,
> Val, the skier's Utopia, cradling champions for
>   over forty years.
> Val, moulding her people to her own image,
>   rough and ready;
> Generations of Val folk founding homes and
>   legends,
> Legendary Val!

The adman and copywriter have arrived in the seventy-five years between these two extracts. So, too, have swifter means of transport, more general spread of money, group travel and, not least in ski-ing, women's emancipation. All modern ski resorts reflect women's participation, in the choice of decor for a hotel to the quality of food in its restaurant. No new resort these days builds rooms without bath or shower – just one more reflection of the feminine influence. Under the strict rule of the Christiana Inn proprietor, women were let in to clean the room, no more and no less. But listen to our Val:

> Dry invigorating air;
> Val in rhythmic harmonisation
>   with the heart beat of existence . . .
> Val-imp night-club haunter,
> Sunny verandahed Val,
> Intellectual bookworm Val
> Val-tonus of the saunas

Val-shopper
Val-eclectic
Bright and friendly Val
Val, Val amour!

Val d'Isère is very dear to me. But it is also the place where most people enjoy a good table at any one of a number of hotels, chat over a beer or coffee and cognac without moving out of doors, and bed themselves fairly early. You will be sleeping at 6000 feet, and until acclimatised you are likely to wake at four or five am and doze only intermittently after that. If you want to clock just a modest mileage of the 195 miles of piste in a ten-day holiday, you need to keep regular hours and forgo excessive alcohol. Most hoteliers offer a Savoie house wine of relatively low alcohol content specifically to help this ambition. It is a place to get to know gradually for, like a good wine, it does not reveal its subtlety in the first tasting. The main street, wide, like that of a Hampshire village or a Colorado mining settlement, is bisected by a river, but in a half-hidden, concreted-off French style. The image of Val d'Isère is set by its people, the families who run the hotels and the staff who greet visitors year after year by their names. The adman's prose scarcely reflects it.

The spirit of the place is reflected in the shrewd use of the neighbouring mountains, with so many fine runs that the beginner may be put off simply by the number of good or intermediate skiers they hear singing its praises (perhaps that is where the copywriter went wrong, too). I took my children, aged twelve and fourteen, for their first full week of ski-ing – they had experienced a few days in Scotland previously – to Val d'Isère and by the end there were two long runs on the Solaise which they could complete. Nor would I recommend Val d'Isère ski school as one of the most advanced. Boy, of course, meets girl in Val d'Isère, but if that is the object rather than the ski-ing, then an Austrian or south Tyrolean wine cellar is a more likely bet.

Each ski country offers a separate experience and style, and within those countries there are further grades and shades of difference. What follows is an attempt to help in the choice of a resort for the first-timer or for one who seeks a bit of a change. The idea, indeed the essential purpose, of this book is to simplify, paring off what it is not essential to know in the first two or three holidays on ski, and this applies as much to the tourist operator's brochure as it does to equipment. After a while skiers develop personal tastes in places as much as they do in skis, boots and clothes. Each will try and persuade you of the rightness of his or her choice, and a convincing personal experience will often influence more than a printed version, however expert the latter may seem. It is not that you suspect a brochure or advertisement of making false claims, but it cannot possibly be objective, for it must exclude the claims of its rivals. The Austrian national tourist office is not in business to promote France, Switzerland, Norway or Italy – and these days the European must add Spain, Yugoslavia, Canada and the USA.

There is the same problem when we are dealing with equipment, but all in good time. For the novice, at least, choice of resort will come before choice of skis. Jenny has a casual boy-friend, Michael, behind whose heavy-lensed spectacles and civil service manner lurks an ambition to succeed at something physical. People with good balance and an ability to slide well are sometimes drop-outs from other kinds of sporting activity. Ski-ing is undoubtedly one of the best levellers, not only among men and women but among men who have habitually captained the cricket and rugby teams and those who have skulked at long-stop and wing. Not too much should be made of this, because good balance matters in most sports, and so does supple muscle. But Michael is just the type who has the application and doggedness to track down the tour operators' shops after his appetite has first been whetted by newspaper and magazine articles.

Newspapers and magazines
Press views and attitudes can be helpful if the writer has a wide experience of resorts and is prepared to criticise and compare, but much writing on ski-ing in the press is superficial and single-track. Journalists, some of them barely able to stand on skis, are invited out of main season to resorts which give them priority and hospitality not available to ordinary holidaymakers. Responsible newspapers should have correspondents able to see through the publicity haze. Whether the resort is geographically sited for reliable snow, and whether the tows have adequate capacity to avoid jams and bottlenecks – these are things which may not be evident when the journalistic party is shown round in early December or even late January. A little waiting around is not a bad thing for the novice, or the skier trying to find his legs for a new season, since it prevents him tiring too quickly and imperceptibly, but long waits mean you get cold and stiff, and not nearly enough value out of a weekly or fortnightly ski pass. These are important considerations, but they do not appear in many press articles.

I am not suggesting dishonesty of approach. Resorts are entitled to promote their interests, just as journalists who cannot ski, or ski just a little, can comment validly on their particular angle. One acquaintance writes only about ski resorts minus the ski, and he is probably better on the après-ski than someone who needs all his rest and energies for tackling the actual runs. On a multi-national trip to Vail and Aspen we started out with fifteen journalists; nine were respectable skiers and better, two had not the slightest intention of ski-ing at all, and four were novices. By the end we were thirteen, two of the novices having broken their legs. They tried to learn without supervision in bad conditions, with lots of new snow and a white-out, which means almost total loss of visibility and no possibility of identifying any bump or hollow in ground even two yards ahead. It was still valid to write of marvellous general conditions in the Colorado Rockies, with powder snow, which can be blown from the hand like thistledown, helping everyone to ski more safely. But most of the newspaper clippings I saw subsequently made no mention of the broken legs which had demonstrated that not even the best conditions can be taken for granted.

Michael, being a careful chap and taking his unofficial responsibilities seriously, should buy the specialist ski magazines in the autumn. In Britain, *Ski Survey*, the magazine of the Ski Club of Great Britain, available free to members or at a modest price from the club, and *Ski*, an independent magazine, all try to sift the information pouring in from tourist offices, tour operators, airlines, retailers, and equipment manufacturers. A genuine effort is made to guide different classes of skier through the maze. Even here there is evidence of one country, region or resort having been involved in a sustained campaign, for the specialist magazines are among the first invited on facility trips. It is no reason to discard what is offered – only to treat it on its merits and inquire about alternatives from the tour operator.

The trouble with ski-ing, and choosing a holiday place in particular, is that everyone providing a service has an angle, an opportunity for personal profit which can affect the judgement. The oil crisis, pell-mell inflation, the failures of major holiday concerns and the introduction of currency, fuel and insurance surcharges have bedevilled costing and choice for the consumer. Many people now visit a tour operator with a pocket calculator to hand. Which tour operator? In the appendix I have listed them, and their specialities where appropriate.

Michael takes this part of the matter very seriously. He collects all the ski holiday brochures in October and early November and piles them on the dining room table. He has a sheet of plain paper to note and compare prices and has gone round a group of friends for views on which country each would prefer. Though most say they think Austria would be best for starters, he is trying to bring an open mind. Currency rates vary widely from country to country. Jenny argues that if they do not book quickly all the best rooms will have gone. Michael, like so many others, wants to wait until December before booking, because by then they will know the exact currency and surcharge situation, and several operators will be offering surcharge-proof terms. Since Michael at this point is doing most of the work, he gets his way. He is going into it slowly and cautiously, aware that each will be spending over £250 on a fifteen-day holiday. For most it will mean a leanish summer holiday, but most have a hankering for a 'doer's' vacation this year. If they do not like it, or find they really prefer a summer laze, they can still find a use for the cold-weather gear they are beginning to think about.

Michael ignores all blurbs advertising holidays from

so many pounds. These are always for the basic price in the guest house farthest from the nursery slopes, maybe without breakfast, at the cheapest time of the season. He is impressed by the brochures which do not try to secure skiers and would-be skiers – on the whole a fairly sophisticated lot – on these terms. The temptation is always to turn to the resorts of which you have heard, but Michael is making a good job of this and is going to compare like with like in various countries. He is helped by those brochures which have a hotel grading system, based generally on amenities. The group are broadly decided on a fortnight at the cheapest time – the middle two weeks of January. Hotels everywhere have four rates, the dearest for the Christmas and New Year fortnight and the middle or last fortnight in February. These are children's and/or public holiday periods in various parts of the Continent and ought to be avoided by any unattached group. Resorts are crowded and worse, so are the ski lifts. The better known the resort the more likely it is to develop queues in high season. Places like St Moritz, St Anton, Kitzbühel, Davos and Zermatt are all famous for the variety of the ski runs once the skier is in the high mountains. But he has to get there first, and while queueing can be entertaining for the show it sometimes offers, that can pall after a while.

The next most popular times are usually the first and fourth weeks in February; then comes the last week in January and the rest of February; cheapest of all are middle January and the second week in March. There are regional variations, usually based on the height of a resort and its capacity for keeping late snow. The purpose-built French stations continue later than most of the Austrian resorts for this reason. The French Easter, or Pâques, is a Government nominated holiday; it is usually in February, well before the religious festival, and should be avoided at all costs. On the other hand Obergurgl and Hochsolden have peak season rates in the first two weeks in April because they are the highest resorts in Austria (Obergurgl is the highest village with a church), and are noted for their late ski-ing. The highest and lowest rates at, say, a three-star hotel in Seefeld would vary by about twenty-five per cent for a room with a bath – a room without bath will save £10 or more, but this can be a false economy, especially in Austria.

Skiers need plenty of baths, not because they get excessively hot and sweaty – their bodies are using up liquid almost as fast as they can put it in – but because the relaxation which warm water gives to limbs and muscles aching in all sorts of unfamiliar places is one of the great pleasures of the day. If you are staying in a small Austrian guest house, or an older hotel without many rooms with baths, you not only have to pay for individual baths at about a pound a time but suffer the irritation of an impatient queue willing you out before you are half done.

It is a bit of a slog, this, but Michael carefully builds up his picture by working through the small print. One by one he checks off the questions:

When was the brochure printed (usually it is March) and what exchange rates applied? In 1976, surcharges for Switzerland rose by as much as twenty-one per cent between March and December.

Bed and breakfast, half board or full board? He soon sees that the hotel garnis, those offering only bed and breakfast, are a good bit cheaper. If it is a smallish Austrian inn on half or full board it probably denotes dinner on the dot at 6.30 pm, not much choice, ample but fairly simple food – lots of pork, veal, and sauerkraut – beer on draught, or light and pleasant Austrian wine. There will be Tyroleans in the bar, amiable, but knowing only a few words of English, which they gladly utter if you give them a German time of day: 'Guten abend . . . Klammer sehr gut' plus a thumbs-up will draw a 'Bobby Charlton . . . Manchester United' and there is no point in going on about Charlton retiring years ago, even if your German can stand it.

Some answers Michael can work out for himself from the printed word. Others, especially on supercharges, are best put to the specialist receptionists which tour operators employ at their main centres. Michael will be looking out for a good receptionist who knows her hotels and will quickly establish the experience and abilities of the would-be holidaymaker. Full board may be preferred by the novice skier, needing a longish midday break from unfamiliar exercise, but it is easy to become sluggish from a big meal and wine. I prefer a snack, preferably on a mountain restaurant's sunlit verandah, and if the group favours a cheaper hotel twenty minutes walk from the nursery slopes it may be better to lunch in a nearby café, snack bar or, in France, a crèperie. All food in mountain restaurants, including those hard by the ski lifts, is expensive, not much less than a downtown lunch.

There are false economies, in both time and effort, in going for accommodation on the outskirts of a village, but there are bargains to be had. For years, British bobsleigh and Cresta enthusiasts stayed at the Eden Garni, an unpretentious bed and breakfast hotel in the middle of St Moritz, paying a fraction of the price the more fashion-conscious, or less knowledgeable, were laying out in other parts of the town. The exchange rate for the Swiss franc is so poor in the 'seventies that nothing much can now be said to be inexpensive in Switzerland, but by its own terms the Eden remained reasonably priced. Soon, too, the more price-conscious discover which bars are used by the locals, in particular the men who

work on the lifts and the mountain pistes. In St Moritz
it is usually Valentin's bar or the ground floor room of
the Steffani Hotel, a huge, bustling, hugger-mugger
restaurant, drinking room and meeting place, which has
none of the artificialities of the Cresta Bar, with its
somewhat overdone Englishness, in the same hotel.

Apart from family groups and crack skiers, almost
everyone's first priority from a ski holiday is a good social
life. The specialist ski tour operators will tell you that the
first question is usually about the evening's après-ski.
After the evening meal, preferably with a cheap carafe
of wine or modestly priced beer, young, single people
want to find a cellar bar or discotheque where they dance
with the same energy as they ski, where a stranger will
say yes rather than no to a dance, where the nationalities
mingle freely and six hours' hard-won sleep is reckoned
to be enough to recharge for the next day.

Once again, the big, well-known resort will be beguiling
with its dozen or more night spots, but even in Austria,
a drinker's country where prices in a weinstube and a pub
are about comparable, a pound will not go far in a
Kitzbühel night club, any more than it would in a
London equivalent. Michael is not put off by this. He
enquires about smaller resorts within fairly easy bus or
taxi ride of the big international centres. So, in Austria,
there are St Christoph, Stuben, Zürs and Lech within
reasonable distance of St Anton, the ski capital of the
Arlberg with its great snowfields, the Galzig and the
Valluga. Kitzbühel, an ancient town, much more a
sightseeing centre than the rather straggly St Anton, is
surrounded by a dozen resorts which in some instances
are closer to the eight major ski areas cloaked in the
Kitzbühler name. So Michael hears of Söll, Wörgl,
Westendorf, Kirchberg, St Johann, Jochberg, Fieberbrunn
and St Jakob. St Moritz is as much a place to see, like

the Prado, or Piccadilly Circus, as to stay in. You can sleep in St Moritz Bad, the original Roman spa, a mile down the hill by the lake, much cheaper than in St Moritz Dorf where the King's Bar at the Palace, Hanselmann's or Hauser soak up rich and casual visitors alike. But there is nothing to stop you wandering around and enjoying the show, and the ski-ing costs the same for everyone. Silvaplana, Celerina, Sils and Pontresina offer less expensive accommodation, with Pontresina very much a place in its own right. Davos has Klosters, Wengen has Lauterbrunnen. And so on.

Michael likes the sound of some of these, but is still keeping his options open. He inquires about smaller, individual resorts, not major centres to the degree of St Moritz or St Anton, but well established and big enough to provide colour and atmosphere, even in mid-January. He hears of Grindelwald and Verbier in Switzerland, Bormio, Cervinia, Sauze d'Oulx and Corvara in Italy, Soldeu in Andorra, Seefeld, Gargallen, Lermoos and Saalbach in Austria. Finally he wants to know about the French resorts, or stations, mushrooming up in the last ten to fifteen years with new ideas and attitudes to the modern skier. Avoriaz, Flaine, Les Trois Vallées, Isola 2000, La Plagne, Les Arcs, Tignes. And should they ignore the second generation French places, Val d'Isère, Courchevel, Méribel? Not quite as new, perhaps they have more character and settled facilities.

At this point it is time to start looking at the expense and how much each in the group can really afford, then at what they are getting for the money. Will it be better to cut the holiday down to eight days and go for something more expensive but more comfortable? They are mainly beginners. Which places suit them best for the money they can spend? What does each country offer in ambience, scenery, weather prospect, convenience and therefore cost of access? How does it affect the package, and what are they trying to sell you? Is a conventional hotel package the best way of doing it? What about chalets? Or bespoke holidays taking your own car? What about currency and fuel surcharges? One week or two?

Taking them point by point, Michael looks closely at the eight-day prices and sees snag number one. Whether for bed and breakfast, half or full board, they will be paying only thirty to forty per cent less for half the time. The flight and other travel costs in all package arrangements is the same for one week or two – about £40 to £50 in 1977. Obviously, then, fifteen days is better value. Snag number two: seven days' ski-ing for the average half-fit Briton means only limited progress. By the time the muscles are toned up for serious progress it will be time to come home. Better seven days than none at all, but if finances can be strained and the time spared, then fourteen days is a much more rewarding period. Above all it gives time to rest and relax between ski-ing. And the whole point of it is recreation – expanding skill and judgment, yes, but enjoyment as well. At times it is a hard, even dangerous, sport. The little stabs of fear, however, help make the skier appreciate the sybarite bath and bar, the jug of wine and the people all around enjoying an intensified existence. Few happily leave that after a week, unless their boots have so skinned their ankles that they cannot get into them at all. But more of that – because it is crucial to the enjoyment of a ski holiday – when we look at equipment problems.

Austria
When Franz Klammer and his successors leap from the start gate of a major downhill race, all Austria lives with them. Grandmothers who have never skied cross themselves, car and portable radios blare a commentary, those

who are able huddle round the TV. Life in major towns and villages comes almost to a dead stop for the two minutes of a Saturday lunchtime World Cup downhill race. In no other Alpine country does the emotion and mystique of ski-ing express itself in such personal and widespread terms. It is, in many ways, a conservative country, particularly in the Tyrol, and followed well behind the Swiss in the development of the winter sports industry. There were two formative figures, Matthias Zdarsky, who first attempted to adapt Norwegian cross-country ski-ing to the much steeper Alpine terrain, then Hannes Schneider, who at St Anton in the middle 1930s developed the stem christie as the chief form of turn.

The first British parties were arriving at about this time, but the Anschluss, Hitler's take-over of Austria, checked this, and the war obliterated ski-ing as a tourist industry. Russians and French converged along the Inn River in 1945, and Innsbruck Station in 1955, on my first journey to Seefeld, was still pitted with cannon and bullet shell. Austria's renaissance began with the reconstruction of the tourist industry, and all who yearned for a return to normality put their hearts and bodies into the effort. While the Germans nursed their wounds, the British came in large numbers, an exchange rate of seventy-two schillings to the pound in 1955 going a long way with a half-litre of beer costing about five schillings and the price of a fifteen-day package by rail about thirty-three guineas. They were not the public school and university Britons so active in the British ski scene, but young serving people from the war who had learned the rougher tricks of travel and danger, and were well able to look after themselves in less testing circumstances. Many Austrians were glad to see them and a relationship developed which survives strongly, especially away from the major tourist traps.

You cannot, of course, be grateful or sentimental for ever and every weekend now, the autobahns from Germany pump non-stop streams of cars into the Austrian mountains. The invasion is more friendly and, far into Sunday night, the ski-packed cars pour back to Munich, Nuremberg and points north in a feelered glow-worm procession. If that sounds daunting it is as well to remember that Austria has well over four hundred officially listed ski resorts, and many car-borne Germans will happily lose themselves among the places – perhaps two-thirds of the whole – with modest facilities and prices to match. Most will be fairly regular visitors, and though the Deutschmark is one of the world's hardest currencies, even that cannot be spread around endlessly. The Briton, on his once-a-winter ski holiday, may feel a poor relation when he sees the Mercedes and BMWs in the ski village car parks but, comparatively speaking, he is going to spend more in his hotel and the weinstube than many of the Germans.

In 1945, Austria had only twenty-five cable cars, mountain railways and ski-lifts. Now there are more than 2500. She has only two resorts in the Alps's top fifteen in pure altitude terms – Hochsolden at 6857 feet and Obergurgl at 6266. But in the middle area, from 2000 to 5000 feet, there is an embarrassingly wide choice of resorts with good, varied medium runs from half a mile to a mile. Medium is a word which constantly recurs about Austrian ski-ing, and that is part of the attraction for a beginner. There is big ski-ing in places like St Anton and Zürs, but many trails wind through wooded glades or across the alms, the mountain farmers' sunny shelves and meadows, testing for the expert if he is taking them non-stop at speed, but pleasant, also, for the less able and less experienced.

In a geological sense, Switzerland dominates the Alps

with its great high central peaks. Austria, slowly sliding
away into the plains of Hungary, has a more relaxed,
almost feminine physical beauty. It is like a giant pear-
drop on its side, with all the best known – and much of
the best – ski-ing in its western provinces, from the
Vorarlberg in the extreme tip, eastwards through the
Tyrol into the provinces of Salzburg and Styria. For the
car-borne, or the adventurer who can bargain without
the help of tour operators, there are marvellously removed,
almost untouched resorts in Styria and the provinces of
Upper and Lower Austria. In general, the runs get
shorter and the snow less certain as you get farther east,
and touring ski-ing, or ski wandern, becomes increasingly
popular among the Austrians.

The wish to convey a friendliness is more important
in Tyrolean Austria than the meaning of words, certainly
in the smallish ski village where life retains an attractive
simplicity. English will be spoken by most of the ski
instructors and those close to the tourist scene. It is
perfectly possible to attend a village function, as I have
at Seefeld and Schruns in the Vorarlberg, not far from
the Swiss border, and progress only by limping restaurant
German, sign language and wide smiles. School French
in this environment is as useful as Gaelic or Urdu. The
Austrians hereabouts are content that you have come to
enjoy their mountains, although many still reap a hard,
unremitting living. Behind the figures in the brochures
are the villages of the Rhaetians, Walsers, Illyrians and
the Germanic tribes who at last gave up their nomadic
lives in the Middle Ages. Not all is sweetly romantic.
From the Tyrol, the German army sucked in men,
however reluctantly, to fight and perish in the Norwegian
and Russian snows. It is not all 'Sound of Music',
glühwein and lederhosen. But anyone who skis, whether
from Earls Court or Didsbury, must quickly get to know

contending sensations, of pleasure and fear oddly mixed and a constant challenge to complacency.

Over the years Austria has struggled to maintain a unified ski teaching system which takes account of changed knowledge and equipment. The Austrian association of professional ski teachers was the first in the field in 1927, and professional wisdoms, notably those of Stefan Kruckenhauser and Fritz Baumrock, have been enlisted for the exposition of the Austrian Ski System in book and diagram form. The balance organs and co-ordinates are among the most difficult subjects to pin down with words and diagrams, and the Austrians have sometimes been mocked for a certain pedantry. But they persist, and in Chapter 7 I will try to sum up the main points of their teaching, together with the French Ski Evolutif and the similarly based American GLM methods. St Anton and Kitzbühel have some of the finest instructors anywhere in the world, not least because of their love of ski-ing. Many of them speak good instructional English, they know how to demonstrate, and their minds are on their pupils rather than their lunchtime beer. The worst Austrian teaching will be casual, but national stereotypes are dangerous. The Tyrolean is a different human animal from the Viennese, as a Scot will differ from a Devonian. Even the Tyrolean village, while apparently looking much the same, in detail may be markedly different, depending which of the tribes developed it. The Austrian, though, has a flair for making something new – whether a chalet or a ski style – appear part of something older. Spontaneity and a gift for enjoying the moment do not always go with efficiency, but that they prefer to leave to their Swiss or German neighbours. Many British, with an inbuilt suspicion of clear-cut pattern and organisation, are well enough suited, and those that are maddened by it have other choices.

Switzerland

In the middle 1970s, Switzerland's excellent marketing organisation was reporting that their severest potential competitor at the top end of the British winter sports market was the fortnight in San Francisco with a week's ski-ing in the Rockies at a cost of about £300 – the same as for a fortnight in a good hotel at a top Swiss resort. It is a situation which has only grown worse for the Briton. The second hardest of hard currency countries might have the lowest inflation rate in the western world, but when people see their own currencies severely downmarked in relation to it they tend to look elsewhere. Duty-free Scotch at Geneva airport at twenty Swiss francs is not worth humping back to Britain when it can be bought more cheaply in a supermarket at home. Yet, bizarre as the economics have become, British winter sports visitors still spend close on half a million nights in Swiss hotels and pensions. This compares with the record post-war peak of 760,596 in 1962–3. A big drop, certainly, but a considerable trade for Switzerland still.

Related to a further piece of statistical evidence, that only forty per cent of winter sports holidaymakers are handled by tour operators, a pattern builds up. The British who go to Switzerland do so in large numbers under their own steam – some go by car, others by special service flights with the Ski Club of Great Britain, the Combined Services or other travel club or employment groups. Many families have switched to chalet living, or negotiated their own terms with smaller family hotels, mostly in low season. Often there are traditional reasons. Some familes have been going to Mürren, Wengen, Andermatt, Davos, Klosters and Villars for half a century or more, and generations pass on their contacts and know-how. Each of these places has a British racing club, the Kandahar at Mürren, Downhill Only at Wengen,

White Hare at Andermatt, Mardens at Klosters and Davos, and Visitors at Villars.

Beginners without family or social contacts can find the frankly middle-class aspects of Switzerland a little off-putting. From its beginnings Switzerland owed much to the British professional and business classes who brought their attitudes, literacy and ideas of recreation to its slopes. The rules of modern slalom and downhill racing were evolved by Sir Arnold Lunn in such company at Mürren. Byron, Shelley, Ruskin and D. H. Lawrence wrote of Switzerland, summer and winter, and the conquest of the high Alps by mountaineers such as Edward Whymper added immensely to the adventure and the literary store. Mountaineering in Victorian times was an antidote to materialism, and for many there must be the same escape in today's ski holiday. The Swiss, being strongly materialistic in their business lives, have an excellent instinct of what to provide and what to leave.

Anyway, there is no pretence that it is not catering for the 'quality' end of the market. There is a strong, state-backed insistence on value for money. Rather than reduce standards – which would be almost impossible in any case, and not even desirable with so many Germans and Swiss natives able to pay the prices – Switzerland has pressed the eight-day package and the chalet holiday. New resorts such as Verbier, Anzere and the Lotschental have arisen, more discreetly than in France, but basically with the same motive of quartering people higher in the mountains where the snow lies, rather than in the valleys where traditional farming villages and hamlets have simply adapted themselves.

In 1965, when I first visited the Regina Hotel, Grindelwald, under the domineering peaks of the Eiger, Monch, Wetterhorn and Jungfrau, the tea dance was crowded with largely English groups, casually if expensively

dressed. In the evening they either changed into evening
jacket and long gown, or went in pullovers and slacks to
the beautiful, timbered secondary restaurant with its
panoramic views of the mountains. In the lounge one
reminisced with the incumbent of the C of E church
within eyeshot down the valley. British currency regula-
tions killed all that. Alfred Krebs, one of a dynasty of
Swiss hoteliers, switched to a grottoed swimming pool
and sauna for the afternoon après-ski, turned his down-
stairs bar with live trio into a discotheque, and continued
to draw a more cosmopolitan set of guests. He went on
advertising every day of the year in the Personal columns
of the *Guardian, Times* and *Telegraph*, partly I suspect, out
of a sentiment which no Swiss hotelier would publicly
admit under pain of the rack.

Swiss ski-ing can be truly big ski-ing. The adage,
'learn in Austria, ski in Switzerland', has an element of
truth. Certainly a skier who has only known Austria
needs to graduate sometime to the Parsenn, above Davos
and Klosters, and Gornergrat, above Zermatt, if only to
return to the warmth of his old love. Swiss weather can
be more severe, and the height of the passes approaching
resorts like Andermatt and even St Moritz can give them
a pleasantly remote atmosphere. The variety of language
and culture – Romansch in St Moritz, Swiss-German in
Grindelwald, French-Swiss in the Valais – is matched by
notable changes in terrain. In the west the cantons, or
provinces, of Berne and Vaud provide rolling, well-
wooded hills with some variable family ski-ing. The
Bernese Oberland of central Switzerland can be as severe
as it sounds, with the artillery crack of avalanches echoing
off the sheer slopes of the Eiger range, while St Moritz's
sky already suggests the intensity of a Mediterranean
blue. Architecture, too, is pleasantly varied, even to the
Spanish feel of the Engadine around St Moritz.

The hotels of Switzerland will produce good coffee, freshly-baked rolls and reasonably interesting food – and so they might with French, Italian and German culinary cultures to call on. Swiss wine, like Austrian, is easy on the palate, and both not only grow wine but drink it habitually. Switzerland, indeed, is the biggest importer of burgundy in the world. Unlike most Austrian wine, which is best drunk out of the wood and swigged like beer, Swiss white wine from the Valais – the vineyards stretch up almost to Zermatt – can be of goodish export standard. Fendant and Johannisberg are two favourites, although Neuchâtel produces a good rosé. The red of both countries is lightweight, but acceptable, the white is especially welcome after a hard day's ski.

As an income earner, tourism rates even before watch-making and machine tools in Switzerland, and hotels are nationally registered and regulated for price and quality. There is less of the Austrian do-as-you-please. There are bars rather than weinstubes, often run by a woman who will have 'bought' it from the hotelier or restauranteur owning the premises and will run it according to her own style and personality. This may be efficient and hard or smiling and chatty – both will be equally businesslike. Swiss hoteliers believe in getting to know their guests, and year after year, it seems, the same concierge will faithfully arrange that you are picked up at the station by the hotel truck or sled, driven by the man who did it in Arnie Lunn's time. Mountains breed loyalty and long life. It is quite wrong to think of Swiss hotels as impersonal, except possibly some of the great Victorian edifices built for the nineteenth-century leisured classes and convalescents. Austria escapes these because most were built in the South Tyrol, which was acquired by Italy after the 1914–18 war. Switzerland soldiers on with them, but they are not truly representative.

France

No Alpine ski-ing country, not even Italy, offered such a
lonely prospect for the British in the 1960s as did France.
Paris, yes, Brittany, yes. In the days of incarcera-
tion by currency restrictions the British would get across
the Channel for a summer break, even if they had to
swim for it. But France and ski-ing existed only in the
sports pages, where the more observant might have
noticed the French winning sixteen of the twenty-four
medals at the World Championships in Portillo. The
Grenoble Winter Olympics and Jean-Claude Killy's three
gold medals brought a wider recognition of France's
ski-ing possibilities, and a relaxation of currency restrictions along with the devaluation of the French franc
suddenly brought Val d'Isère, Alpe d'Huez, Courchevel,
Megève, Les Deux Alpes and others into the tour operat-
or's brochure at a more realistic level. French tourist
publicity, all but non-existent for years, began flickering
across the Channel and when Flaine, a brand-new resort,
staged the British Ski Championships in 1972, it was a
small but significant sign of the changing times. British
investment went into Méribel before the war, helping to
change the nature of recreational ski-ing, and now it has
gone into a radically different centre, Isola 2000. British
skiers are slowly following. To too many, however, France
south-east of Bourg St Maurice and Grenoble is unknown.

The modern French ski image is more an ocean liner
than a Concorde. George Cumin, in a paper called *Les
Stations Integrées*, which outlines the development of the
French ski station, relates the self-sufficient theory behind
it to 'une paquebot des neiges'. From flat to hotel,
shopping centre to swimming pool, creche to discotheque,
there is everything needed for a 'ski cruise'. Most of the
early resorts, between 1000 and 1500 metres, had a
season of about three months and were a ski centre

grafted onto an existing village. Development was piece-meal and unco-ordinated but, as in many Austrian villages, often worked in a pleasing, haphazard way. The problem was lack of snow in variable winters.

Sestrière, built in the Italian Alps in the late 1930s, was the first purely purpose-built resort; Fiat, the motor company, provided a model for the later French stations with access roads, accommodation and ski lifts balanced according to need. Courchevel, after the war, was collectively planned, but followed conventional ski resort lines with traffic, pedestrians and skiers mixed; the lessons of Zermatt, Mürren and Wengen, where there were natural obstructions to cars, had still not been learned. These second generation stations, as they came to be known, include Val d'Isère, Alpe d'Huez and Megève. Whatever their other virtues they tend to sprawl and to be without a focal point.

The third generation, for example Flaine, Avoriaz, Les Arcs, La Plagne, Pra-Loup, Les Menuires and Isola 2000, are on different lines still. Because of altitude or favourable situation – there are distinct snow pockets – a snow arena can be made central to the architectural plan. It is the assembly area for beginners, a meeting place for friends ski-ing together, the start and finish of all runs, and is close to the lifts. This site is selected before the main buildings are planned.

At Flaine, only 400 metres separate the farthest hotel or apartment from the first lift. It is a horseshoe of five hotels and eight apartment blocks, with a second stage of 170 flats, for renting only, sixty metres above and connected by lift. All modern French resorts have used a famous ski name, for example Emile Allais at Flaine, Jean Vuarnet at Avoriaz, Honoré Bonnet at Pra-Loup, to design or advise on ski facilities. The French gift and tradition for civil engineering looks at the way skiers want to behave and adapts the facilities to them, not the other way round. It has revolutionised the sport, for other countries have had to revise their ideas accordingly.

It was the French who developed the widespread use of automatic tows. The skier pushes a slim bar, which opens like a gate at knee height, triggering the release of the tow bar. The skier settles the disc or soup plate, about nine inches in diameter, between his legs, relaxes his knees and, after a phased interval to allow him to settle himself, he is automatically pulled to the top of the run. It did not entirely do away with manning, but it meant a single operator looking after a tow cluster. The old weary waiting while individual tow owners painstakingly clipped or tore off sets of tickets – still the case in some parts of the Alps – was superseded by the abonnement, a season ticket for all lifts within a given area. It was not only cheaper, especially for the intermediate and advanced skier who could safely ski a variety of runs, but much reduced waiting time. It also brought about lift clusters, fanning out from a single starting area over a variety of mountain faces. More uphill capacity put ever larger numbers of people on the slopes, and the need grew for Snowcats and Unimogs, the tracked vehicles capable of ploughing up hard-packed and potentially dangerous pistes and of resurfacing where bottlenecks of skiers reduced the track to rock and ice.

Some people are taken aback by their first sight of a French apartment-orientated ski resort. At Tignes, the blocks are as pretty as piled kitchen utensils. The alloyed roofs, a protection against heavy snow, gleam like saucepanware. Apart from the aesthetics the advantages are real. Self-catering is much cheaper. Unsightly external features may be useful amenities, like exclusive balconies, catching every available ray of the sun. Foldaway tables, beds and chairs create living space for much larger numbers than the apparent size would indicate. Families thus ski much more economically than if they stayed in hotels. Most come by car from Paris, Lyons and other city centres, but slowly the British are catching on, and excellent road-clearing services reduce hazards although you still need snow tyres or chains. Chains can be hired at valley towns like Bourg St Maurice before the high Alps are reached, but few people travelling from Britain can hope to time their arrivals to ensure that garages are open. Geneva by air or, perhaps best of all, French Railways from Paris to Bourg, are other approach routes to the main cluster of resorts in the Savoie.

La Plagne is among resorts widely advertising flats for sale, offering to service and let them when the lessor does not personally want to ski. Britons have to pay a premium for this kind of property, as for any other. To give some idea of self-catering in France, as opposed to hotel living, the 1977–78 cost of an apartment at Flaine sharing with four others is about half the price of a stay at a three-star hotel. There are big savings on bookings through specialist operators, who can throw in cut-rate fares packaged with reduced apartment rentals. The Swiss are also strong in this field, primarily through Swiss Chalets Ltd, but France has pioneered the flatlet conception, as well as the opportunity to buy a particular apartment over a period of years.

French ski-ing, then, has a distinctive style and flavour. Some hotels, for example the Savoyarde in Val d'Isère, are recognising changing needs and offering big cooked breakfasts until eleven am and an evening meal, assuming skiers will prefer to break briefly for a snack at lunch on the mountain. But lunch is France's main meal, it is a traditional and conservative country in its eating habits, and other nationalities may expect to see the mountains clear as if by a fairy wand at midday. Especially is this so at resorts like Megève and Alpe d'Huez which are catering heavily for people who do not ski. In general the standard of ski-ing at Val d'Isère, Courchevel and the more intensively mechanised higher resorts is good. French ski hire equipment is of a notably high standard, most shops using the more expensive range of Rossignol skis. The fixing of bindings is done with care, and although it may be a bit off-hand if you choose a peak Monday morning time, that can apply anywhere.

A word of warning, however, about the Latin countries in another respect. The Ski Club of Great Britain insurers, Douglas Cox and Tyrie, with an experience stretching over twenty years, find France and Italy much more of a risk for stolen skis than Switzerland or Austria. It is partly geographical, partly because the French ski hirers do often let a good and costly article. I had a pair of hired Head Master Skis stolen from a hotel ski room in Alpe d'Huez, refunded the maximum of £50 under my insurance, and was still faced with a demand for a further £30 three years later. It required the involvement of the French Tourist Office and the regional Syndicat d'Initiative to arbitrate that no used ski at that time could be worth as much. Business is very much business for the French hire shop. In 1975 I had a further pair stolen from the ski room of a French apartment block in the few minutes while I went to get the ski locker key, which was also needed for the flat. I had arranged a special additional insurance cover for this eventuality and could pay the £60 demanded. In Chapter 6 I shall look at insurance matters more closely.

France's other major breakthrough has been in ski instruction. The majority of the new resorts now teach Ski Evolutif, a method evolving also in the United States, where it is called the Graduated Length Method (GLM). It is practised principally in France by Robert Blanc at

Les Arcs, a 1970s resort 120 miles south-west of Geneva and bursting with new ideas. I deal with Ski Evolutif in more detail in Chapter 7 but briefly, it means the system by which total beginners start with skis only a metre long and progress to 1·35m and 1·60m as soon as they get the feel of sliding on snow. Skis are always kept parallel, and within a fortnight beginners may be taken on 'ski sauvage', which sounds what it means, ski touring away from the crowded pistes. Les Arcs has its own radio station, giving details of weather, snow conditions and the day's entertainments, and a free internal telephone service (your room number is your telephone number). A moving staircase up through the village enables the better placed to ski home through their windows. One of the night clubs has a pit of black glass as a dance floor and tables are at four levels so that every party is separate and intimate. It is a whole new ski scene, distinctly and – for some – overwhelmingly French.

Norway
The taste for Norwegian ski-ing and life style is, I suspect, more deeply shared by the British than by any other European neighbour outside Scandinavia. The tragedy is that Norway's hard currency has made holiday incidentals extremely expensive. There are ways round, as the British-Norwegian Ski Club (See Appendix: Clubs, etc.) has found, but travel might be thought arduous if you sail, as many still do, from Newcastle to Kristiansand in the deep south or Bergen on the west coast. From Bergen to the nearest well-known resort, Voss, is 100 miles by rail, and from Kristiansand to Hovda 125 miles. To my mind the voyage, even across a turbulent North Sea, beats flying any time, and is all part of the holiday. Flights are available, however, to Bergen and Oslo.

Norway's tallest peak, the Galdhöppigen, is 7000 feet

compared with Mont Blanc, the highest in the Alps at 15,771. The northerly latitude ensures more snow but a lower tree line. In American ski resorts like Vail and Aspen, on the same latitude as Sicily, fir trees will grow to a height of 8000 feet. In Norway it is 3000 feet or less and, though the Gulf Stream provides considerable warmth to the west coast, a switch of wind to the north in mid-winter brings down Arctic winds of considerable severity. The sun in mid-January is low on the southern horizon and the days short. On the other hand the Scandinavian high-pressure zones are a notable meteorological feature, bringing a light so clear that snow glitters like crystal and colours are wonderfully enhanced. Norway is best visited when the days begin to lengthen.

Norway has eight Alpine centres, and if the country is imagined as a mutton chop suspended by its narrow end, all are in the fat part except one, Narvik. The Bergen-Oslo railway line bisects the mutton chop section laterally. On the line, working west to east, are Voss, Geilo, Gol, Hemsedal and, in the Oslo area, Norefjell. South of this line are Kongsberg and, in the Setesdal area, Hovda. Above the line, about an hour and a half's journey south of Trondheim, is the remaining resort, Oppedal, home of many of Norway's crack racing skiers, both Alpine and Nordic.

The qualification of a Norwegian Alpine resort is that it must have a vertical drop of 700 feet, be mechanically prepared and be served by at least two lifts. It must have facilities for ski school and for renting Alpine equipment, and a catering establishment of reasonable standing at the foot or at the top of one of its runs. At least thirty places satisfy the vertical drop requirement. To put it another way, if an imaginary plumb line were dropped from the highest point at which the runs begin to the finish of the shortest, the length of the line must be 700 feet. In practice, all runs wind down a mountain at considerably greater length than the vertical drop. For example, the men's Olympic downhill run at Innsbruck has a vertical drop of 870 metres, or about 2700 feet, while the run itself is 3145 metres, or two miles. A Norwegian vertical drop of 700 feet will give runs of half to three-quarters of a mile, a little longer than equivalent Alpine places because the land will fall more gently. On the other hand there are truly steep, tough slopes at places like Oppedal and Voss. The wild, precipitous peaks of West Norway tower 6000 feet above the fjords. If the Alpine skier looks for challenge, he can find it.

Norwegian ski-ing, however, is rooted in its Nordic traditions. Here Alpine ski-ing is primarily for the young, touring ski-ing is for everyone. It is the means of getting around with the greatest economy of effort, a constant interplay of downhill, uphill and flat. It is skating, gliding, climbing, with light flexible skis of wood or glass fibre, supple boots which could almost be used on a squash court, and bindings loose so that heels will be free for every swing forward. At its best, it is the nearest sensation man gets to flying. In the early winter Norwegians ski in the forested trails around their homes. On Sundays, up to 100,000 of Oslo's population of half a million will take to the forests and the 1200 miles of marked trails of Oslomarka, the 1000 square miles of natural park girding the city. Anything up to ten miles is quite normal for old or young, male or female. A Norwegian loves to take his visitor into untracked snow. 'Stop,' he will suddenly say. 'Listen to the silence.' And silence it is, broken only by the sound of snow falling from a fir branch, by the rustle of a bird or snow animal.

The Norwegian likes to get away to the higher ranges as spring approaches, so that he can leave the trails (many of them floodlit close to towns or big centres) and reach the Vidda, the high plateau where he loves to be his own navigator and where, map and compass in hand, he can track every variety of snow and crust. Broken limbs are an exception; indeed most insurance companies offer a one-third discount for Norway, not simply because the national health services are reciprocal with Britain's but because accidents are so rare. Hardanger is the biggest of the Viddas, one hundred by sixty miles, most of it above 3000 feet, and ideal for the nomad who loves the snow desert life. Norwegians take it in groups, knowing exactly where the refuge huts lie. Britons may get the hang of Nordic ski-ing within about a week, but they should not attempt this sort of thing for at least two or three visits, and then only with a guide at the right time of the year. January and February storms can be fierce, and the sub-zero temperatures can easily bring on frostbite. I suffered a frostbitten thumb idly ski-ing at Geilo. I made the mistake of popping a frozen thumb in my mouth, and though I wiped it quickly the heat loss was conducted rapidly. The thumb blistered within a few days, as if I had scalded it, and full feeling did not return for a year or more. Rubbing the thumb hard on a piece of dry trouser material would have been more sensible.

Late March or early April are good times to visit Norway, providing it has not been a freakish winter without too much snow – at one time such a winter was unknown and is still a rarity. Newer hotels are usually clean-lined, with wood and textured interiors to please the modern eye. The Norwegian cold table, with its amplitude, variety and display of fish and meats, sits well in these circumstances. Even better if, as is likely, the hotel dining room looks out onto a wilderness of snow, frozen lake, pine forest and undefiled massif. Women's dress at dinner is more formal than at most Alpine centres. Alternatively, huts, spelt hyttes, can be hired for

any period. Usually they contain a living room with a
kitchen annexe, two or three bedrooms with bunks,
electricity, heating and running water. They are comfortably furnished and cleverly designed, the cost varying
from £30 to £60 a week at current exchange rates.
Easter brings the great invasion – from Sweden, too – of
Norwegian resorts, large and small. Prices double and it
is a time the foreigner should avoid.

Ski-ing is the national sport of Norway. It was a
Norwegian, Fridtjof Nansen, who saw the modern world's
need of escape into snowbound wilderness and possible
danger when he wrote, in 1888, in his classic, *By Ski over
Greenland*: 'If there is anything which deserves the name
of sport of sports, it is surely ski-ing. Nothing hardens the
muscles or gives the body power and suppleness as it
does, and nothing has the same ability to keep the spirit
so fresh. Is there anything healthier than to take your
skis on a frosty winter's day and speed into the forest?
Is there anything finer than our Nordic landscape when
the snow is softly sprinkled, feet deep, over forest and hill?
Is there anything that gives such a sensation of liberty
and excitement, of flying like a bird over wooded slopes,
while winter air and pine branches rush by your cheeks,
and eyes, mind and muscles are strained taut to avoid
unexpected obstacles? Is it not as if the whole burden of
civilisation is suddenly washed from your mind, to remain
in the polluted city air you have left far behind? It is as
if you are one with your own ski and nature around you.
Ski-ing nourishes both body and spirit, and it means
more to the country than most people suspect.' A little
romantic for St Moritz or Megève, or perhaps for many
tastes in the latter half of the twentieth century, but in
Norway, as you look out over the Jutenheimen (the 'Home
of the Giants'), the central mountain range of Norway,
the lyricism can still seem relevant and appropriate.

If in my earlier account of my first visit there I gave the impression of Geilo as some kind of Colditz, then I apologise deeply to a country of which I am inordinately fond. If Fleisher's hotel at Voss, just up the line from Geilo, does not still have a string trio playing Grieg, Coward and Lehar at tea-time, with people relaxing amid the ferns after a hard day's ski-ing, then I am truly sorry. If the cocoa and whipped cream in remote ski huts is not made slowly with melting bars of chocolate, then Norway's patience – even with skiers such as me – is not what it was.

It was Norwegians of the last century who turned ski-ing into a modern sport. Nansen's *By Ski over Greenland* gave the world its first inspirational ski-ing literature. Sondre Auverson Norheim, a sad but epic character, in Morgedal, southern Norway, arrived at the ski shape, binding and technique which is still extraordinarily close to that of today. Norwegians invented wax and the laminated ski. They introduced ski-ing to the Americas, and if miners skied to the pits in Weardale, England, two hundred years ago, then it was the Norwegians who taught them. Half of Norway is uninhabited mountain range, not mountains thrown up by major upheavals, but ground out by glacial activity. Stark, timeless massifs stand out above rolling plateaux, great forests of conifers, frozen lakes and lonely fjords. From Kristiansand to the North Cape of Norway, is as far as from Kristiansand to Rome in the other direction. There are only four million Norwegians, and two-thirds of them ski. They are kindly towards Alpinists, and offer admirable facilities, but their terrain invites them never to ski down the same hill twice. They taught me the plough turn which took me safely up into the Vidda, where a mountain horizon opened which will never foreclose.

Italy

Italian resorts are a slowly rising commodity among centres served by British ski tour operators. Their relative neglect may be more a commentary on traditional British tastes than on the standard or variety of ski-ing on the southern side of the Alps. Things are changing now, with the lira and the pound equally low-valued and new routes carved through the Alps, but distance remains a factor.

Italy had more reliable snow than many central and northern Alpine resorts in the late 1960s and 1970s. Pista and pasta are compatible, as anyone who has lounged outside the imposing, south-facing hotels of Pocol, at Cortina d'Ampezzo, will know. The Mediterranean sun burns with a particular intensity, the sky this side of the Alps has subtle gradations of blue and turquoise, and the sensation of a vineyard or orange grove just beyond the next spur provides a sensuous atmosphere which only France begins to share. It would be too self-indulgent and sybaritic for a sport as challenging as ski-ing if it were not for the Italian character, colourful, boisterous, self-aware. 'Prego! . . . Avanti!' the British bob team would shout at Italian males preening down the slopes at speeds well short of the dangerous. It was all good-natured. Eugenio Monti could well look after Italy's reputation for daring and skill on the nearby bob run.

Most Italians contentedly ski the well-manicured pistes which keep Italy's accident figures well below the average, retire for lengthy luncheon sessions with Campari and Chianti to augment their lasagne and cannelloni first courses, and leave the tourists and children – lots of them everywhere – to sport during the lengthy siesta period. Nowhere is the sea-beach scene so successfully transferred to the snow as at an Italian resort on a fine weekend. It is important to emphasise week-end, for ski-ing is still very much the activity of the Italian middle-class townsman,

up from Milan and Turin, except in the South Tyrol to
the east, where peasant and farmer enjoy the mountains
much as do their Austrian neighbours to the north. Many
of Italy's ski racing champions have Austrian antecedents
– Gustav Thoeni for the most part speaks a gutteral
German.

Italian ski-ing is much bigger than its reputation. The
Italian Alps are not a fringe mountain area quickly
descending to plains – indeed, there are more Alps in
Italy than in any other country. In the east, the Dolomites
encircle the remote Leydin valley and its resorts of
Ortiséi, Selva and Corvara. The jagged precipitous peaks
are of limestone magnesia rock which, when iron is
present, illumines the great massif in a lustrous pinkish
glow. It is one of the wonders of the geological world.
A skier can rest on his sticks in this remote loneliness,
beautiful and wild in the same context, and marvel.

These resorts are more for second and third year skiers,
and until the completion of the Brenner autobahn were
comparatively inaccessible, with Munich a long, tiring
coach journey away, Innsbruck avoided by most of the
major airlines because of the encroaching mountains, and
Venice the best approach by air and an eighty-mile coach
journey. Now it is possible to reach the Sella mountains
from Calais or Ostend with one overnight stop travelling
almost all the way by toll-free autobahns. A journey by
Airo Alpe single-engined plane from Cortina to Milan –
another possibility by scheduled services – through the
valleys of the southern Alps was one of the most awesome
I have undertaken. Sitting next to the pilot, with clouds
banking up and visibility often nil, I knew something of
the spirit of Jim Mollison and Amy Johnson. Happily the
pilot knew his way blindfolded.

Moving west, in the central Italian Alps there are
Livigno and Bormio, just over the border from St Moritz.

Livigno lived in isolation so long that it became known as 'Little Tibet', and it retains a distinction in being a duty-free area, which ought to be set against its comparative inaccessibility. A tunnel from the north has made it more available but it retains much of its old character. Bormio has something of this remoteness in physical terms, but it was a spa in Roman times and is more town than ski resort, with lift journeys necessary before the slopes are reached. To the far west, completely different in style and tone, with the French influence strong, are Sauze d'Oulx, Sestrière (the original purpose-built resort), Cesana and Claviere, whilst closest of all to Geneva, reached easily by the Mont Blanc tunnel, is Courmayeur. Although Courmayeur is a little low if snow is short, the Italian side has suffered less than the rest of the Alps in several recent winters.

Spain and Andorra
The most popular country for British overseas summer holidays is, by some way, at the bottom for winter sports. Understandably so, since it came as a surprise even to Spaniards that in Francisco Ochoa they had a slalomer good enough to win an Olympic gold medal at Sapporo in 1972. Ochoa is the son of a hotelier at Navacerrada, a dozen miles north of Madrid in the Guadarrama, but for practical purposes Spanish ski-ing is confined to the Cantabrian and Pyrenee range on the northern border with France, and the Sierra Nevada in the south. These are mighty ranges, still in the early stages of ski development, but with great possibilities.

Pyrenee ski-ing is from 2700 metres (7300 feet) to 1500 (4600) and includes the small (sixteen miles by eighteen miles) but independent-minded principality of Andorra. From east to west, the best known resorts are La Molina,

Masella and Nuria in the Catalan Pyrenees, and Candanchú and El Formigal in the Aragan Pyrenees. Soldeu, one of the best known resorts in the Pyrenees, is in fact in Andorra, where the official language is Catalan, direct taxation is non-existent, and whisky is £1 a bottle. It has runs up to 2000 metres long on broad fields and easy beginner slopes.

La Molina was the first of the Spanish resorts in 1945, most of the others having been custom-built in the last ten years or so. Spanish ski-ing is relatively cheap, well organised and good for the beginner to intermediate. Drink – other than sherry – can be bought more cheaply than in any other ski country in Europe, which is no bad thing since night life, other than discotheques, is relatively limited. In general the peseta, like the lire, has weakened with the pound.

Much ski-ing is above the tree line – and therefore vulnerable to wind – or dodging among small bushes, though there are long trails through wooded glades in places like Masella, near La Molina. Lunch follows the usual late Spanish tradition – 2 pm to 3.30 – so some settle for a long morning ski and leave it at that, but dinner is from 9 to 11, leaving rather too much time in the afternoon for the cheap booze. It is perhaps best to go rather early or late in the season, when the sun is at its warmest and the days long. The runs can become crowded at weekends, but Barcelona is 150 miles from the nearest resorts and Zaragoza, the other airport terminal, 90 miles. By some Alpine standards there are no wild crushes, but the French from the north and the Spanish from the south are coming in ever larger numbers. The road route to Andorra is via Aix-les-Thermes and Hospitalet (N20 from Paris) or via Puigcerdá when the pass at Col de Puymorens is closed. Since Andorra petrol is duty-free for the return journey, a car holiday has advantages – the Andorran border is approximately 600 miles from Dieppe.

With the opening of Granada airport, Sol y Nieve, a purpose-built complex at 2000 metres on the Sierra Nevada, is the most southerly resort in Europe. Ski-ing in a bikini is perfectly possible, with the Veleta and Mulhacén reaching up to 10,000 feet and retaining snow as late as June. Most of the ski-ing there is above the tree line on slopes which are bold and striking rather than beautiful. During the spring it is possible to swim in the Mediterranean and ski the Sierra Nevada, ninety miles from the coast at the nearest point, on a combined holiday. Ski instruction in Spain generally is said to be reasonable, with forty instructors at a place like La Molina. At Soldeu, in Andorra, most of the instructors are British or North American. Ski hire and instruction, plus lifts for a week, cost about £30 in Andorra in 1977, and rather more in Spain.

Chapter 3

The British Scene

For over forty years Britain has competed in the Low-landers' Ski Racing event, more recently staged in Val d'Isère, against Denmark, Holland and Belgium. A few years ago the Danes started bringing in some distinctly un-Vikinglike competitors with flat, broad faces and slanting eyes. 'Ha, Greenlanders!' one observant, if less than tactful, Briton exclaimed one day at the committee table. 'Not exactly Lowlanders, are they?' 'Ah!' said a Dutchman, 'but what about your Scots? Will they nae go back to the Heelands?'

Britain is no longer a lowland nation in ski-ing terms. Twenty years ago Scotland was for the ski-ing brave. Over their fifth double malts, veterans ramble on about the two-hour treks from the Glenmore Lodge camp site across mountain torrents spanned by single tree trunks, over icy stepping-stones and perilous deer fences, before the first snow could be reached. They still had to climb step by step, sometimes on skis sheathed with skins, before the pleasure of a run down. Even then the mist might descend, damp and eerie, to remove every pleasure from the experience, or the wind swing from gusty south-westerly to northerly, and bring horizontally driven hail from the Arctic to scour the skier from exposed slopes as effectively as shell fire.

Scotland can be arctic. Reindeer survive there off lichen when in the Alps they would die. But it is mountainous, as any relief map indicates – three-fifths of the land is over 750 feet. The only doubt, and it was a very large one in the 1950s, was whether it was tameable, whether all the capital expense and effort could ever justify the return. The answer, by the middle 1970s, was a most emphatic yes. In twenty years, ski-ing on a true seasonal basis, from January 10 to the end of April and later if the snow lingers, has come to be established in the Spey Valley area, based primarily on eight villages, Aviemore, Grantown, Carrbridge, Nethybridge, Newtonmore, Kingussie, Boat of Garten and Kincraig. Dominating the valley to the east is the great massif of the Cairngorms, with Cairngorm itself not the highest of the peaks at 4084 feet – Ben Macdhui, to the south-east, undeveloped as a ski area, rises to 4296 – but the queen of these particular ski slopes.

It required an enormous act of faith, greater than the business judgement, some would say, to provide the services that can be found today, with many others on the drawing board. At the top of the Ptarmigan ski tow, nearly 3600 feet up on Cairngorm, it is possible now to look down on fourteen ski runs, four chair lifts and seven ski tows. Instructors from six ski schools will be working on pupils of all ages. On a busy weekend, with good snow down to the car parks at Coire Cas and Coire na Ciste, there will be upwards of 6000 people spread over the various faces. Britons who have known only Continental ski-ing, seeing this for the first time in good conditions, have to pinch themselves to believe it is true. When wind and weather allow, lifts can take up more than 10,000 skiers an hour.

Of the two chief Cairngorm grounds, Coire Cas was developed first, in 1962, but Coire na Ciste's two major chair lifts and 2717-foot tow, established in 1974, have revolutionised the area. Not only did they double the downhill capacity for intermediate skiers in a notably protected, snow-holding corrie, or valley, but they opened up all sorts of alternative possibilities. 'It's a new dimension,' Bob Clyde, the general manager of Cairngorm Sports Development Ltd and one of the pioneers of modern Scottish ski-ing, enthused. Sometimes the worst enemies of Scottish ski-ing are the Scots themselves, deeply divided on many issues, including the style of market, pace of change and cost of almost everything. Although many hate the architectural and commercial compromises of Aviemore itself, a holiday centre for summer and winter, they acknowledge the springboard it gave to the entire conception of a Spey Valley ski area. The Aviemore Centre was built where the rough road to Loch Morlich carved the first path from the A9 eastwards to the mountains. These are snow-dappled into late May, the corries retaining snow fifteen to thirty feet deep, long after the combination of gale and spring sun would seem to have cleared the old, raw-boned, but still majestic mountains of their skiers' runs.

There are three main Scottish ski areas, Cairngorm, Glencoe and Glenshee, of which the first is outstandingly the most important since it sets out to cater for all classes of skier all week throughout the season. Scotland has a number of other potential ski mountains, notably Ben Wyvis, north of Inverness, at 3429 feet gleaming above the Moray Firth and usually with a bountiful snow covering in winter and spring. It has few of the rocky outcrops bedevilling many other Scottish mountains, but this extraordinary Shangri-La is at present thought too far from population centres. Conservationists also resist strenuously every ski-ing development, not necessarily for the ski-ing itself but for the support services – hotels, shops, roads, lifts and so on – which development entails. Cairngorm's growth was only achieved after violent, and, in some areas, continuing battle with conservationists.

Scottish weather
I remember boarding the overnight sleeper at Euston for my first trip to the Highlands in 1967 with no less pleasure and anticipation than on my first trip to Norway, Austria, Switzerland, France and the Rockies. I had no idea what to expect of Scottish ski-ing beyond Monarch of the Glen poster conceptions and a warning from my Scots editor that it could get pretty cold there. It was the first British Ski Racing Championships ever to be held on Cairngorm, and probably one of the most successful ever.

It was April, the sun stayed out virtually all week, just enough snow had lingered, the Aviemore Centre was still relatively uncommercialised, and the lions of early Scottish ski-ing, people like Hamish Liddell, Lewis Drysdale, Guy Chilver-Stainer, Frith Finlayson, Karl Fuchs and Bob Clyde, held court in a different hotel or pub every night. A hired car made nothing of the thirty-mile round trips inevitable for a genuine tour of the inn- and pub-based Scottish after-ski. Malt whisky and mountain water were the gentlest combination for any festive occasion, and Scotland was declared a resounding success by most concerned with that particular occasion. It was a holiday I would recommend with confidence given weather half as good. Several more visits showed the one-star Scotland more often – overcast skies, buffeting wind, beaten heather and boulders from the White Lady tow and Shieling (café-restaurant) down to the Coire Cas car park. It is offputting to arrive at a ski centre without the slightest trace of snow – and that, usually, is Aviemore Centre – and a Scotch mist concealing the hills to the west and the much higher range to the east. After that

the surprises are more likely to be pleasant than unpleasant.

The Post Office now receives more than 100,000 calls
annually from skiers all over the United Kingdom
inquiring about conditions in the Central Highlands.
Many Scots will listen to BBC and IBA television and
radio snow condition reports, which are broadcast nightly,
and Glasgow Weather Centre also services Press Association in London so that newspapers can print the information if they choose. Many do. The obvious course for
anyone wishing to ski a weekend is to watch the snow and
weather reports in the daily press during the week, then
after 6.30 pm on Thursday or Friday, depending on travel
arrangements, make a final check with the 'Ski-ing
Information Bulletin' taped on the multi-line telephone
number, 031–246–8041. The service is publicised in every
telephone directory in the UK and the bulletins will
contain the full version of snow reports from Cairngorm,
Glencoe and Glenshee. Alternatively, those travelling by
car can pick up Friday night reports from BBC Scotland,
Radio Clyde, Radio Forth and Radio Durham, all of
whom try to get the information into their 6 pm news.

Even the bulletins need some interpretation. Regular
weekend skiers will know that 'vertical runs 1000 feet' on
Cairngorm means that the White Lady will be skiable
from the top of the White Lady tow to the Shieling, but
there will not be anything below that. Many potential
skiers with as much as a 600-mile return journey may be
put off because of uncertainty with the terms. It is worth
a closer look, then, at what they are and how they were
arrived at.

Before the winter of 1964–5 no ski information scheme
operated anywhere in the British Isles, and that includes
Scotland outside the immediate Cairngorm, Glencoe and
Glenshee areas. The use of binoculars and imagination

was occasionally obvious in the few reports reaching national dailies, official weather reports from the Meteorological Office were too general, there being no Central Highland station in the network, and in any case only forecasts were offered when skiers required both prospects and existing conditions. The Scottish National Ski Council, formed in December 1963, got things moving. In 1965, Donald McNaughton, then head of the Glasgow Weather Centre, thrashed out a scheme with the Council and the ski lift operators at the three main centres and it is the basis of the present arrangements operated by H. A. McKellar.

Each day at 4 pm through the winter season a representative of the ski lift operator will telephone Glasgow Weather Centre with a report in two parts. The first is on weather, the second on snow. Weather will give details of wind direction and speed, air temperature, visibility, cloud amount, type and height of base, humidity and details of any current or recent precipitation. They are reports of general value to the weather pattern and are fed into the nationwide network. The snow reports are more specifically a service to skiers, but must be made according to a strict code, as follows:

Snow cover	*Nature of surface*
1 All runs complete	1 New snow
2 Most runs complete	2 Powder snow
3 A few runs complete, others broken	3 Spring snow
4 A few runs complete but narrow, others broken	4 Wet snow
5 Only one high-level run complete, all others broken	5 Very wet snow

6 No complete runs, snow cover patchy

7 Ample nursery areas

8 Limited nursery areas

9 Very little or no snow

Qualifying terms

1 With many icy patches

2 With icy patches

3 On a hard base

4 On a firm base

5 With a breakable crust

6 Drifting (at the time)

7 Drifting badly (at the time)

8 With moderate drifts (drifting over)

9 With deep drifts (drifting over)

10 No remarks required

6 Hard-packed snow

7 Surface icy

8 Windslab

9 Very little or no snow

State of access roads

1 Clear

2 Icy

3 Slight snow

4 Moderate snow

5 Deep snow

6 Moderate snow (drifting)

7 Deep snow (drifting)

8 Very difficult because of drifting snow

9 Blocked

The reports will also add, very importantly, the maximum vertical descent available without break in the snow cover, e.g. 'Vertical runs 1500 feet'. The top of such a run is taken as the highest point to which skiers can be transported by chair lift or ski tow. On Cairngorm this would mean the Ptarmigan at the top of the White Lady chair lift, which is at 3600 feet. The Shieling at the bottom of the White Lady lift is at 2550 feet, so anything over 1100 feet means that the White Lady and Coire Cas runs are complete, and the more protected Coire na Ciste, too. Finally, reports will give the snow level, though this can change so rapidly that it can only be general. It is always more applicable to the corries, where the snow accumulates, rather than to bony spurs which are often bare of snow. Glenshee and Cairngorm have sought to name specific runs and their snow cover, but it was found impossible to pass correct spelling of Gaelic names to the Post Office at Edinburgh and Press Association in London.

The changeability of the weather, and with it the condition of the snow, is best tracked by the freezing level, which is sometimes, though not always, given in reports. In terms of temperature variation, 100 feet in Scotland equals 1000 feet in the Alps. The freezing level can yo-yo wildly, particularly in the evening after thawing all day. Black ice on the access roads has brought many an unwary motorist to grief early or late in the day. Similarly, skiers can go from powder or 'boiler plate' (hard, crusty snow) at the top to 'crud' (sticky, rotten snow) at the bottom.

Newspapers are forced to condense some of the information for space reasons, but taking Wednesday 10 March and Saturday 13 March from the *Guardian*, a picture can be built up, making use of the codes and the weather maps from the paper. The maps of some daily papers have no isobars – the lines joining regions of the same pressure – or arrows giving movements of pressure systems, and are of little use to the amateur forecaster. He will be trying to make a decision on whether to commit his weekend well before the professionals are prepared to commit themselves, and a study of the weather forecasts, snow conditions and maps is essential.

Scotland gets most of its low pressure from the meeting of cold air masses from the polar regions and warm air masses from the south. The cold masses tend to move in a westerly direction and the warm in an easterly. When they meet there is a great deal of turbulence, for warm and cold air have different densities and do not mix easily. Cold air tends to curl round the back of the warm mass, and a depression, marked 'Low' on the maps, and perhaps several hundred miles across, is created. The cold air moves faster than the warm and eventually forces it upwards. The two wedges of cold air come together and all that is left is a slowly revolving mass of cold air. The depression is then occluded.

Scotland gets both a great many depressions and a great deal of rain, falling as snow on higher ground. Partly this is due to air being forced to rise to colder levels by the high land lying in its path, which is relief or orographic rain. Partly it may be due to warmer air riding up over a mountain of cold air, in other words depression or cyclonic rain. Or it may be a mixture of both. Certainly those depressions over northern Scotland or the Orkneys are likely to bring snow to the Cairngorms in the winter and spring, but they may also bring a scouring turbulence. The closer together the isobars the higher the winds are likely to be; the converse also applies. Winter high pressure, as in the examples, brings little or no rain, the possibility of fog early and late in the day, cool temperatures, but a prospect of good sunshine, which the skier will enjoy if the snow cover holds. According to the examples it is a bit warm and getting rid of the snow too quickly for the weekend at Glencoe and Glenshee, but a depression front is coming in with the probability of rain or snow. And so it proves. Glencoe does best with most runs complete by Saturday 13 March, powder snow on a hard base. Cairngorm skiers need sharp edges for the ice they encounter up top.

As a final check on weather and snow conditions, it is possible to telephone any one of the three centres.

The frustrations in Scotland's weather are many. Philip Rankin, managing director of White Corries Ltd, which runs Glencoe, can see masses of snow to a great depth

Northern Ireland, N. Wales, NW England, Lake District, Isle of Man, SW Scotland, Glasgow : Cloudy with occasional rain or drizzle. Sleet or snow on high ground. Wind S. fresh or strong. Max temp 8C (46F).

W. Midlands, NE and C N England : Bright intervals at first, soon becoming cloudy with occasional rain or drizzle. Some sleet or snow on high ground. After early frost. Max temp 7C (45F).

Borders, Edinburgh, Dundee and Aberdeen : Mostly cloudy with occasional rain or drizzle, sleet or snow on high ground. Wind S. strong. Max. temp. 6C (43F).

Central Highlands, Moray Firth, NE and NW Scotland, Argyll : Mostly cloudy with rain at times, sleet or snow on high ground, brighter later. Wind S. strong. Max. temp. 6C (43F).

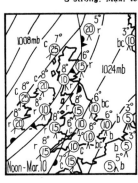

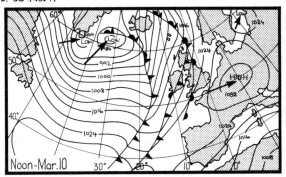

NW England, Lake District, Isle of Man, Cent N England, SW Scotland, Glasgow : Cloudy, with rain or sleet at times and snow on high ground. Wind N fresh or strong. Max. temp. 5C (41F).

Argyll, NW Scotland, N Ireland ; Mostly cloudy but mainly dry. Wind N fresh or strong. Max. temp. 5C (41F).

NE England, Borders, Edinburgh, Dundee, Aberdeen, cent Highlands ; Mostly cloudy, with rain, sleet or snow at times. Wind NE strong. Max. temp. 5C (41F).

Moray Firth, NE Scotland, Orkney, Shetland : Mostly cloudy, with occasional rain, sleet or snow. Wind E fresh. Max. temp. 4C (39F).

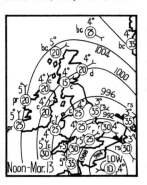

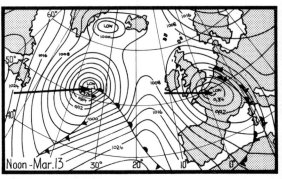

Fig. 1   Weather maps.

associated with easterly or southerly fronts and depressions then, perhaps, have a succeeding north-westerly scour it all away again. Bob Clyde on Cairngorm can have every run complete but the wind so strong that he dare not operate his chair lift or tows. The record, in 1975, was 140 mph. Or, as frustrating, the approach road up from Loch Morlich is blocked with snow so that no-one, not even the operators, can get to the bottom of the chairlift and make use of all that white gold! In fact Cairgorm Sports Development are also responsible for the clearing of the road, an astute move all round which tends to get things moving quickly.

More likely than any of these possibilities is the game of dodgems, not so much with the Scotch mist, which will give reasonable visibility, but with the low-lying cloud of varying density – the infamous 'white-out'. Cloud lifts and falls on Cairngorm with such feyness that locals are ever ready to play the tow-lines. As cloud drops on the Cas, so the Ciste fills up as people switch. It's all in the Scottish ski game. Everyone has his or her Scottish ski story. My own was peeling off the White Lady tow just as the clouds came down. My companion, Peter Emslie, well familiar with the mountain and our destination, which was the race course on Coire na Ciste before the chair lift was built, hailed me to follow him left. Within five yards he was swallowed by the mist. White-out, the term to describe lack of identification of any feature of ground or sky, was total. The wind further numbed my senses. I took a precautionary turn, to see if my legs were responding, and fell over. I picked myself up, cursing, and set off again. I had to be able to turn. This time it was a wide stem christie. Again my legs turned to lead and I fell. Suddenly the mist lifted and comprehension dawned. I was in more or less the same place as I had started. That was not me moving, that was the wind going by! Fall you will if you try to turn while standing still.

Scotland has reasonably up-to-date equipment hire services (five in Aviemore alone) and you can buy practically everything you can get in an Alpine resort, including Veilhaber skis made in the village. Spare gloves, hat, anorak (or knee-length cagoul) and trousers are advisable. It does sometimes rain horizontally, either on the mountain or as you come off it, and snow turns to rain. Hotels are invariably equipped with drying rooms, and regular skiers get themselves plastic boots, though some maintain that the leak-proof boot has yet to be invented. You often change in difficult circumstances half in, half out of the car.

There is ample accommodation; hostel, B and B, farmhouse, rented cottage, for those wanting to live outside the 'developed' areas. Apart from Christmas, New Year and Easter Holiday (the Scottish season is late), the visitor arriving unannounced rarely fails to find a welcome at one or other B and B sign. You can join a club, but it is rarely worth it for a short visit. Scottish Ski Club huts offer a homely welcome and are frequently used at all the three main centres on payment of a day fee.

It is possible to tour the Scottish hills, and the trip from east to west Grampians across the Central Highland massif is quite frequently done. But the deaths of several children on an adventure expedition and of a straying skier in 1975, plus avalanches in 1976, have led to strong safety propaganda. It is unwise to tour unless accompanied by local experts; it is not so much the touring which is difficult but the judgement of highly volatile weather conditions to which the skier might be exposed. The Scottish Nordic Ski Club, based in Aberdeen, is encouraging all forms of touring and competition, and is also busily promoting ski orienteering, in which competitors find their way by compass and map to a succession of checkpoints.

At the heart of Scottish ski-ing is the National Ski Council, with more than 9000 members in 60 clubs, providing racing, training and coaching, and a basis for the entire activity. Through Scotland and the artificial slopes the British have a serious, dedicated scene. 'Outdoor education' means not only British instructors for British holidaymakers but a ladder of training and coaching which, increasingly, can take youngsters to a highly sophisticated level of performance. Up to 5000 skiers enjoy their sport in Britain daily for a four-month season. Weather permitting, never a weekend goes by without junior and senior races taking place in Scotland. About 600 ski party leaders and 400 BASI (British Association of Ski Instructors) have passed through Glenmore Lodge courses, and will influence ski development throughout Great Britain. Courses continue throughout the Spring. Hugh Hunter-Gordon with his Scottish colleagues, established a computerised seeding system which was adopted by the International Ski-ing Federation, and Scottish ski racing has domestic rankings to which all British skiers can relate. It provides not only a pecking order for start lists but a yardstick by which a young skier can judge progress. The SNSC has excellent insurance schemes, to cover loss of equipment as well as accident on a Scottish mountain, and continuously watches the interests of holiday as well as competition skiers. The novice at Aviemore will derive much comfort from this geared, aware scene.

Cairngorm
The pioneers of individual enterprises in the granite villages have retained their suspicion or dislike of the

much larger business interests which produced the Aviemore Centre of concrete hotels and piazza at Aviemore, the Post House Hotel, the Coylumbridge and so on. In truth, the skier goes there to take his pick of a whole variety of hotels, guest houses, pensions, caravans and tents, in a package where a Bank of England or Bank of Scotland pound note is not going to be skinned by the exchange rates, then drawn and quartered by a cup of coffee or a glass of beer. He can share the warm huggermugger of the Struan House Hotel, where Karl Fuchs, an Austrian international skier, settled down in 1954 with his English wife, Eileen, to produce a successful blend of Austrian-Scottish ski instruction, a son who could reach the top twenty in world downhill ski racing, and a dialect quickly recognisable in this part of the world as Scostrian, with its peppering of 'unds' and 'mits'. Hans Kuwall, another Austrian, is chief trainer for the British Association of Ski Instructors, the Scottish National Ski Council's chief development officer, and runs the Hillend artificial slope and Carrbridge Ski School. A home-grown Scot, Frith Finlayson – a wiry, red-haired shipyard worker from Glasgow – developed the Ski School d'Ecosse to the power that it is.

The Post House, Strathspey, Badenoch and Coylumbridge (on the road to the mountain) offer multi-star accommodation for those who want it, and in the 1970s it was all put on a professional footing with the Spey Valley Tourist Association banding together more than forty hotels and guest houses for various forms of package deal. With the active help of the Highlands and Islands Development Board, they are now artfully put together to encourage the traveller from down south, whether from Glasgow or Edinburgh, Manchester, Bristol, or London. Putting the plus side first, there is a wide spectrum of accommodation, with prices naturally lowest for guest houses farthest from the ski slopes – which in Scottish terms means up to twenty-five miles, albeit over quiet, easy-motoring roads. Scottish food is plentiful and whole-some, with huge teas including scones and baps thrown in for those who want to dodge a bit of slope time or are put off by the weather. Travel is relatively easy. The M1, M6, A74, M74, M73 and A80 provide dual carriage-way from London or the south-west to just short of Crieff.

The M9 makes a confident start across the Forth to Glen Farg, but then adventure begins on the old A9 via Pitlochry and the Drumochter Pass, although the new oil way to the north now by-passes Dawwhinnie. This is still motoring out of the 'thirties, and if a blizzard starts to blow you listen to your engine beat, look for traces of a recent snow plough, wish you had packed a shovel and some sacks, and start thinking of survival drill if you should skid into a ditch. It can still be a bit like that from January to early March, but ordinary motoring common-sense ought to be enough for most contingencies, and ski-ing never was for the faint-hearted who wanted to stay that way.

The novice skier is well considered, with 'Learn to Ski' packages providing six days on the slopes. Lowest prices are quoted for 'own car' arrivals, with additions for rail and air transport (primarily to Inverness, transport laid on from there) carrying useful discounts. It is only fair to warn that in the late 1970s costs have been rising by twenty per cent annually, which still compares favourably with much of the Continent. Prices are usually based on one person sharing a double room, with six days' ski instruction, hire of skis, sticks and boots, unlimited use of chair lifts and tows, and ski bus tickets from hotel or resort to the slopes. Reflecting the American and Conti-nental developments in self-catering, there is also now the Freedom Inn at Aviemore, providing a compact suite with cooking and dining facilities for a family group, plus the amenities of a large hotel. The Aviemore chalets provide a cheaper, more basic form of self-catering, with meals obtainable at the centre.

Speyside Valley arrangements are made through Ness Travel, 32 Academy Street, Inverness (tel. 39481). There is also an information officer at Aviemore 363. Arrangements do not provide for insurance, though this is recommended in spite of the national health services immediately available whereas they are not on the Continent. Ski accidents frequently require quick, specialist treatment followed by remedial care and, regrettably, theft of skis remains as possible in Scotland as it does in Austria (not a big chance, perhaps, but a chance). Deposits of £10 are required per person and the balance of fares must be paid six weeks before a holiday. The Weekend Ski Club, 6 Kew Green, Richmond, Surrey (tel. 940 7782) has excellent arrangements for long weekends involving rail high-speed coach travel which youngsters at any rate seem to take in their stride; the club ought to be consulted over longer stays, too.

You have to like Scotland for its basic rawness, for timeworn rock and determined fir and heather, for sudden vistas through lifting clouds, for lochs which provide mirror and sheen unlike any mountain scenario I know. If on the other hand Aviemore Centre, with its pin-tables and go-karts side by side with ski shop and boutique, alienates the determined Alpinist, I must confess that the tables and cars whiled away many pleasant minutes for my children, then aged ten and eleven, on their first five-day ski holiday in 1973. The indoor pool and ice rink were equally appreciated, as was the artless, ramp-like artificial slope and ski hire arrangements, though the skis had obviously struck rock and heather as well as snow.

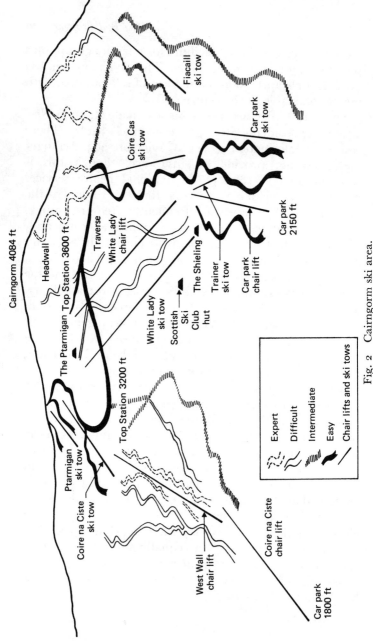

Fig. 2 Cairngorm ski area.

Cairdsport at the Centre have burgeoned with the short ski method and claim that it has revolutionised teaching at Aviemore, with novice pupils on shorter, slightly wider skis usually progressing from the beginners' slopes at the bottom of Cairngorm by the middle of the week. Seven-day rates here, with four hours ski school per day, ski boot and stick hire, and unlimited use of chair lifts and ski tows, are £40 for an adult and approximately twenty per cent less for a youngster under seventeen. The Cairdsport method is not exactly the Graduated Length Method or Ski Evolutif, which introduce longer skis over a fortnightly period, because of difficulties with terrain, snow and available learning time, but it makes use of the principle.

Nursery slope ski-ing on the bottom runs is liable to frustration due to sudden thaw. I took my children right to the top, on the shallow and easy Ptarmigan tow, after the bottom runs melted almost literally under their feet. This was all right until the hail started pelting down, and the swimming pool made a far better alternative to ski-ing. This, I must add, they accepted quite philosophically as part of a quickly changing scene, the nature of which they perceived and understood as readily as adults. The alternative amusements at Aviemore Centre were perfectly acceptable to them over five days.

The £250,000 Coire na Ciste development, begun in 1974, could point one answer to the beginner problem. The art of positioning six-foot high protective snow fencing is well established among the Inverness road engineers. The same art has been applied with the installation of 6000 feet of fencing to the new Monaich run on Coire na Ciste, this time to conserve snow rather than to keep it from trouble spots on the road. The new Ridge Race run, the 'M1', has a further set of parallel fences, 100 feet apart and 7000 feet long, and even from

Grantown on Spey, fourteen miles to the north as the eagle flies, the new pattern of snow conservation can be seen. More fencing on the beginners' slopes served by the Car Park and Trainee tows beneath the Shieling should preserve snow longer there and enable skiers to run down to their cars more easily.

The 1977 day-ticket charge for the Cairngorm lifts was £3.50 (peak period £5) and going up twenty per cent yearly. Beginners may find a transferable, any-day, ten-coupon card more flexible, but it was not cheap at £4. Single trips for major tows were 50p for an adult, 30p for a child. For the many skiers coming up regularly from England, membership of a Scottish ski club, with lift discounts of up to twenty per cent, is clearly a bargain.

Aviemore, Britain's only ski-ing resort, is as proud of its après-ski as is any Continental resort. Allowing that après-ski can mean something like midday if the conditions are truly disagreeable, this is an important and, in my view, justified boast. The ideal Aviemore holiday is a week, though continuously favourable snow conditions would make a longer stay perfectly valid. With the help of local experts I offer suggestions on places to visit:

Winking Owl Nest Bar. Fine selection of malts. Haunt of many instructors and ski bums. Friendly staff. Excellent bar lunches and snacks but a bit on the small side. Jenny and Michael would both be happy here.

High Range Tavern. Small and comfortable, friendly atmosphere, and a change from the trendier places. Good bar food.

Illicit Still. Spacious, lively bar at the Post House. Trendy furniture, piped music, but good folk night on Sundays and disco on Thursdays. Tailor-made for Jenny.

Cairngorm. Modernised bar in the Cairngorm Hotel, the one established big hotel before the Centre was built. Very comfortable. Dartboard.

Cluny. Part of the Strathspey, meant to be the poshest of the two original Centre hotels (the other is the Badenoch). Bar still suffers a bit.

Viking. Blaring basement of the Badenoch.

Alt-na-Craig. Where locals meet. Smoky, small, but the place for the heaviest sessions. Dartboard if there is room. Michael will like it.

Deerstalker. Part of the Centre complex, lacking a bit in character, but noisy on dance nights.

Struan House Hotel. Not to be missed, especially if Karl Fuchs is presiding. Strangers can easily join the circle of this extraordinary British–Austrian gemütlichkeit whae hae.

Outside the USA and Canada, Scotland is the place where freestyle ski-ing has taken perhaps its deepest root. Most weekends of the Scottish season, freestylers offer a free show to novices and intermediates pausing in their own activity. Freestyle, or Hot Dogging as it is sometimes known, was developed in North America as an escape from the tradition and techniques of Alpine racing. 'Doing your own thing' was all very well, but it needed a few rules. In the first competition in Colorado in 1971, one competitor raced down the hill doing only six turns. Another, just to be different, spiralled down doing a thousand turns.

The 'horizon stretching' has settled into three main

forms – mogul run, ballet and aerials. Mogul ski-ing has
kept much of its original form, with fast, aggressive ski-ing
down a steep, bumpy slope, but judges now score more
highly for control. Ballet ski-ing is close to figure skating,
with a routine scored to music and careful choreography.
In the aerials, upright jumps and somersaults have been
codified – the spreadeagle, the daffy, the twister, the
helicopter, the back somersault and so on. Eleven
thousand spectators watched Manfred Kastner perform
the first triple somersault at Snowbird, Utah, in 1971.
Aviemore in 1977 saw a series of competitions for the
British Freestyle Championships sponsored by Colgate,
and many found it a better spectacle than racing.
Everywhere, now, better skiers on short skis are trying
some of the tricks. Freestyle is clearly here to stay.

Glencoe

The most westerly of the three main Scottish ski centres,
Glencoe lies 78 miles north of Glasgow on the A82 in a
setting of magnificent scale and brooding beauty. Glencoe
is the vale, Meall a Bhuiridh (3600 feet) the highest
mountain of the region. Apart from the peak periods of
Christmas, New Year and Easter the tows operate at
weekends, when all are welcome. However, a group is
able to hire the whole mountain – the only place in
Britain where it can happen and the Ski Club of Great
Britain have done so. Thirty people can have exclusive
use of the mountain on a Friday or Monday at a cost of
about £5 each. They will obtain limited running of the
access chair lift up in the morning and down in the late
afternoon. On top they can have use of either two T-bar
tows or one T-bar and a chair lift. The chair lift's top
station is next to the Scottish Ski Club and commands one
of the finest views in Britain across Rannoch Moor into
the heart of the Grampians and across to Ben Nevis. It is

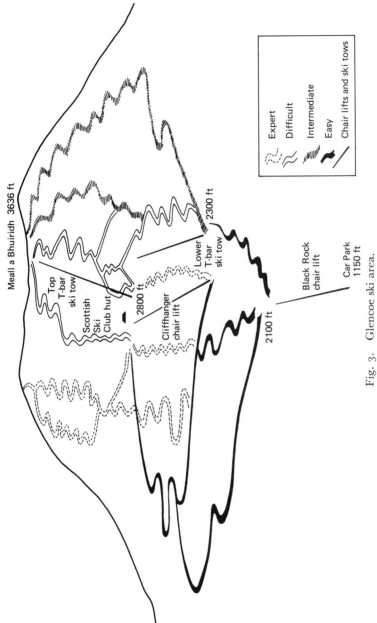

Meall a Bhuiridh 3636 ft

Top
T-bar
ski tow

Scottish
Ski
Club hut

2800 ft

Lower
T-bar
ski tow

2300 ft

Cliffhanger
chair lift

2100 ft

Black Rock
chair lift

Car Park
1150 ft

Expert
Difficult
Intermediate
Easy
Chair lifts and ski tows

Fig. 3. Glencoe ski area.

a sight well worth the effort even of a non-skier. Such a group can ski there still on Saturday and Sunday, paying normal rates, but accommodation in the immediate area is limited – at the Kingshouse Hotel nearby from March onwards. The A82 from Glasgow is one of the most scenic in Europe and, having been built by Italian prisoners of war, has a few built-in autostrada ideas. For information, telephone the White Corries Chairlift Company (Balachullish 303).

Glenshee

The twenty-mile stretch of the A93 into the hills to Glenshee from Blairgowrie (fifty-five miles north of Edinburgh via the A90) has been improved over the years to create slightly better access, and there is more accommodation than at Glencoe. Together with the Spittal of Glenshee and other hotels in the glen there are the Fife Arms and Invercauld in Braemar, and a number of smaller hotels in Blairgowrie with appropriate facilities for skiers. Five-day holidays, inclusive of breakfast, dinner, ski instruction and hire, were being offered at £35 plus VAT in 1977, and self-catering at £20, which had to be about the cheapest in Europe (EBA Ltd, Dingwall 2462). Glenshee was once approached by the famous zig-zag of the Devil's Elbow, though this has been well graded, straightened and tamed. The main uphill transport from there is a chair lift up the 3059-foot Cairnwell with tows to either side of the main road. When there is reasonable snow cover a wide variety of runs to the west of the road forms a circus using the Cairnwell chair lift, the Cairnwell Ridge tow, the Butchart's tow and the recent Carn Aosda tow. To the east of the road, leading from the parking areas, the Sunnyside tow services beginners and provides access to the Meall Odhar tow.

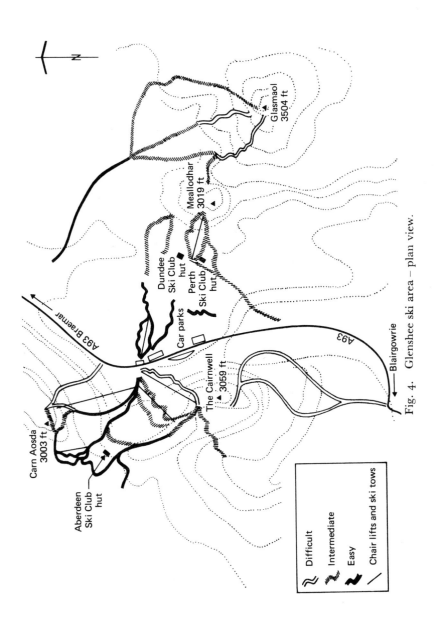

Fig. 4. Glenshee ski area – plan view.

N

Carn Aosda
3003 ft ▲

Aberdeen
Ski Club
hut

A93 Braemar

Dundee
Ski Club
hut ■

Perth
Ski Club
hut

Car parks

Meallodhar
3019 ft
▲

Glasmaol
3504 ft ▲

The Cairnwell
3059 ft ▲

A93

Blairgowrie

Difficult
Intermediate
Easy
Chair lifts and ski tows

ARTIFICIAL SLOPES

Since a keen skier with Dendix, an industrial brush-making firm, designed the first artificial slope with PVC monofilaments at West London in 1961, over seventy have been built to many different designs in fourteen acres of British parks, leisure amenities or spare plots. There are now nearly 500 instructors qualified to teach on these, and many slopes have their own ski clubs. Most of the slopes, though, are readily available to a general public – children as part of school or extra-curricular activities or with parents themselves at the learner stage; family groups training up for winter holidays; people who, having learned, want simply to carry on using the facility; and the competition skier in slalom or freestyle looking for a training opportunity or race practice.

Some of the slopes are public ventures, others private, and the size can vary as widely as the style of use. There are also marked differences in price. The National Ski Federation list is included in the Appendix and shows that, except in northern Scotland, which usually has snow enough anyway, no-one in the UK is much more than sixty miles from a slope. They vary from the 400-metre slope at Hillend, Edinburgh, Britain's biggest, to small indoor ones, including examples of the rotating Mogul slope, an ingenious British invention which has the skier performing on a rollered band, the speed of which can be adjusted to simulate degree of slope. A slope of about twelve degrees is desirable for beginners and up to thirty degrees for the more advanced. A slope nine metres wide will allow two racers to compete side by side down similar slalom courses, events particularly popular among spectators and the young. Bearsden, Glasgow, operates three full racing leagues and on a Friday night up to 300 parallel slalom races are held. At Southampton and a few other of the more imaginatively designed runs, trees and the occasional bump or ridge have been incorporated in the hope of simulating more natural snow conditions.

The better outdoor slopes are floodlit and have tows, which vastly improve the rate of use, and offer courses of five or six lessons for beginners. The price for an hour's lesson varies from £1.25 to £3 depending on whether it is a group or individual arrangement, and less for school or youth groups. Open practice will be £1 to £1.50 and hire of skis, boots and sticks is nearly always included. Reduced rates often apply for courses, which some slopes make obligatory rather than having complete novices stumbling down and being a nuisance or a danger to others. This does require a commitment, of course, and autumn or early winter weather is a deterrent to that. Who wants to ski in a British downpour? Rain speeds the slopes up, as a matter of interest, but that is scarcely the point. All British sport offers some challenge or possible rigour from the weather, so why not ski-ing? Those slopes offering café and bar facilities, or those forming part of a leisure centre with indoor alternatives, are in a much more favourable situation.

The matting used on sixty per cent of the slopes is Dendix, easily recognisable by its toothbrush-like diamonds. They are made of PVC monofilaments clamped into stainless steel channels in zig-zag strips which, placed together, form a diamond pattern. SkiMat, which is used at thirty per cent of slopes, is made of hexagonal rings with moulded plastic bristles and each ring clips into its neighbour. SkiMat is cheaper than Dendix and wears more quickly, but worn sections are easy to replace. There are several injected plastic types: Delta, after its shape; Snomat with a round ring; Sorboski, another hexagonal; and Vango, with bristle of uneven length filling the middle of the ring. These surfaces give the impression of harder packed piste than Dendix. It is a great mistake to use one's own equipment on any of them. Ski soles wear out much quicker than on snow. A good, hard soled ski is much more important than one with edges. Shorter skis are certainly better, and usually a slope's hire skis are fitted with Gertsch bindings, where the plate comes with the ski and boot, to reduce fitting time.

The 'plastic' does not behave like snow, but it has enough of its characteristics to make ski-ing on it a useful exercise or straightforward enjoyment – providing the slope itself is adequately designed. Some of the original outdoor slopes are not, and many of the others could have been much improved by more thought about their function. Many slopes are simply angled hillsides covered in plastic, the earth having perhaps been excavated for another reason, without landscaping or detailed attention to use. 'There is no outdoor slope in Britain with adequate uphill transport,' says John Shedden, the National Ski Federation head coach in England. 'Time spent climbing is relatively wasted time. A skier is there to ski.' He wants the area for class tuition to be as wide as possible, especially for schoolchildren, so that as many as possible can go down together instead of one by one. This area should be treated separately from other ski-ing areas for more advanced skiers. That, it must be hoped, is on its way.

Shedden instances a number of ramp-like structures where inadequate attention to compacting and grassing has meant mud oozing through. Since 1000 square metres of SkiMat, say, is going to cost upwards of £30,000 by the time equipment, storehouse/reception, floodlighting, lift and instructors are added, plenty of care must go into Britain's 'plastic' expansion. But with over 30,000 schoolchildren now ski-ing annually the demand goes up and on and there is considerable re-thinking about the nature of artificial slopes, particularly by John Shedden. The National Federation has a target of two million skiers and two hundred artificial ski slopes, to include at least twenty ski centres with very long runs, plus cross-country tracks linked with biathlon rifle ranges, and small ski jumps. Inter-regional and British international competitions now take place on artificial slopes. With the number of qualified British instructors increasing, there is a growing objection to schoolchildren taking pot luck abroad among possibly inferior teachers who cannot reward them with the three grades of proficiency certificate available here.

Slopes more than 200 feet long include Aberdeen, Brentwood, Craigavon (Northern Ireland), Edinburgh Hillend, Folkestone, Glasgow, Gloucester, Kilmarnock, Kirkby, Alexandra Palace London, Crystal Palace, Sandown Park, Watford, Newcastle-under-Lyme, Northampton, Pontypool, Rossendale, Royston, Southampton, Stalybridge, Telford, Torquay, Tunbridge Wells, Welwyn and Widnes.

GRASS SKI-ING

Ski-ing on artificial slopes is largely a training ground for snow. Grass ski-ing is more an end in itself, and its devotees have grown at such a pace that the Ski Club of Great Britain found it necessary to appoint a specialist secretary. The International Ski Federation (FIS) at its 1975 San Fransisco Congress decided not to recognise grass ski-ing, in spite of strong British lobbying, but FIS at first refused to recognise the rules of slalom and downhill drawn up by Sir Arnold Lunn – they are a notably conservative body. The British have pressed ahead unabashed because it is a type of ski-ing suitable to our terrain and climate.

I must confess to being an early drop-out from grass ski-ing. My first, indeed only, experience was on Parliament Hill Fields, London, in 1969, on the Orville Wright equivalent of grass skis. They looked and sounded like young panzers, and it was hardly a surprise to hear that a German manufacturer of sewing machines, Kurt Kaiser, had thought up this way of making us ski. The amiable young man who was helping market the skis, known as Rollkas, said encouragingly, 'Just relax and take off. If you want to turn, just put your weight on one or the other. Don't try and edge and don't attempt a snow plough. It's easy. Just watch.' And he zoomed down the slope with easy skill as these people always do. I had no arm or knee pads, as they offer the luckier learners these days, and the skis were too short for stability. I tried to traverse, then ran out of hill and had to turn too sharply – a familiar enough defensive attitude in snow. I did not fall, but was too tense to get much pleasure from a little bit of downhill running onto flat. The skis seemed hard to control. I really did not give it much of a chance, like a number of others at the time. We were too far ahead of the revolution.

Far better equipment and instructional methods were on their way. Modern designs are longer, and the Rollkas with caterpillar tracks on nylon runners are capable of up to fifty mph. Grilsons, a British firm, introduced a cheaper ski on rollers in 1972 and it has proved highly successful for beginners and intermediates. The Ski Club now has a twenty-two page booklet on British grass ski instruction leading to Bronze, Silver and Gold tests, just as it has with snow. It has detailed instruction, for example, 'Preliminary Exercises: Lift one ski about a foot off the ground and hold it parallel to the other. Repeat with the other boot . . . Star turn, repeatedly stepping skis to a new radius to face a different direction.' The

Class One instruction, available to anyone who turns up at their meetings, goes on through walking on the flat, climbing, straight running, swinging to the hill, traverse through progressively steepening lines, progression to parallel turning, and lift riding.

The fear factor, so strong in all sports where specific techniques must be introduced in the act of sliding, is rather lower in grass ski-ing where jeans, long sleeves and gloves will protect most from serious damage other than the odd graze or grass burn. In the first five years of the Ski Club seriously taking hold of the sport, there was only one broken leg – when a girl ran through a bunting line and tripped over the wire. There is far less leverage on a grass ski compared to even a short snow ski, and bindings open easily. The edge of a grass ski does not, like that of a snow ski, dig into the snow unexpectedly, throwing the skier off balance (known as 'catching an edge'). One of the few extras necessary for regular grass skiers is an oil-can. The nylon runners can get very hot, and in the early days people got some nasty metal burns. This is a sport Jenny and Michael might be tempted to try before their first snow holiday. Like water ski-ing, the techniques may be somewhat removed, but it does give an experience of planing, of trying to do something with attachments to the feet while in motion. Also, if the instruction is clear and confident the novice disciplines himself to learn, and this can be of value when he reaches the snow.

Skiers do tend to pick it up quicker than non-skiers, which must mean that grass skiers take more quickly to snow ski-ing. The same might be said of water ski-ing. Jane Fawkes of the Ski Club says that the mistake of most snow skiers is that they start grass ski-ing by trying to slide rather than steer their heels. 'We encourage them to bend lower and, to turn left, touch the heel of the right boot with the right hand. They see how easily they go round and it's a major step forward.' Grass skiers use ski sticks with champagne corks impaled on their points to prevent them sticking into the ground. 'You plant your right stick just ahead of the right ski for a right-hand turn,' says Jane, 'Sticks otherwise tend to flap around in a do-as-you-like way.' It will not be long before someone develops a stronger theory than this if ski history is any guide.

The first problem of a novice, as with snow ski-ing, is to get up the hill. Portable tows mostly for grass ski-ing have a motor-propelled cable on to which you clip your metal 'nutcracker'. As soon as the nutcracker bites you are tugged along by the moving wire. The initial jerk takes some getting used to; beginners are often tugged off their feet because they are tensed in a bad posture, usually leaning forwards too much with the bottom stuck out. The secret here, as with snow tows, is to relax the knees and slot the clip onto the moving wire at your side rather than a foot or so in front of the body. After a while you do it almost without thinking, but it is undoubtedly a knack to be mastered.

Grass skiers are not only a thriving doers' community, they provide tremendous Sunday entertainment for the British car poodlers looking for something a bit unusual. There are four national race meetings, several regional ones and ordinary meetings most weekends from spring until autumn. There is now an annual European Grass Ski Championships, but that is for the cracks, and requires a course four hundred metres long with a slope of fifteen to twenty degrees on a smooth, rolling hill.

Ten permanent grass ski-ing sites, used most weekends, are Allenheads (Northumberland), Waterhall (Brighton), Bruton (East Somerset), Burton Dassett (Banbury), Butser Hill (Peterfield), Castell Howell (Llandyssul),

Hillend (Edinburgh), Usk (Gwent), West Wycombe (Bucks) and Windermere (Cumbria). A calendar of events, dates, directions and useful phone numbers is published annually by the Ski Club of Great Britain who will gladly send it, and will answer any other queries from members and non-members. Films are also available for interested groups.

Grass ski-ing is a large, jolly, outdoor activity, with people picnicking from their cars and smaller children and dogs roaming the ample hillsides that usually abut the ski courses. Spectators often want to join in, and are usually surprised that for a pound they can hire boots, sticks and skis and join a small group of other beginners on a nursery slope with an instructor. Lessons are modestly priced, there is no age limit, bottom or top, and the fun is infectious.

A keen grass skier who buys his own skis – the cheapest will be between £25 and £35, the dearest about £70 – can try cross-country ski-ing. One group regularly treks, setting off from Beachy Head and ski-ing the South Downs ridges to the outskirts of Brighton, or across Welsh or Pennine mountain ridges. Some enthusiasts keep grass skis in the car boot, and if they see a good suitable slope will whip them out and try a 'virgin' course. 'Sometimes through the long grass it feels like powder snow,' says Jane Fawkes. The basis of most meetings, though, is a giant slalom and a parallel slalom race between gates, with two racers at a time fighting it out on side-by-side courses. Another advantage is the après-ski – usually the first local pub willing to take a pile of muddy skis at the door. Ski-ing on British grass, like ski-ing on British snow or plastic, is an everyman activity.

Chapter 4

Decision Time

Having decided on a January holiday, Michael and Jenny look at transport. If they go by car they will be better placed to shop around as in January hotels are much less likely to be fully booked. But Michael argues that January or February weather can turn really nasty and he is not too experienced in snow and ice driving. It simply does not happen enough in Britain, and when it does the snow characteristics on home roads are not necessarily the same. British snow is generally warmer and wetter than Alpine.

Jenny is more tempted by the idea of a car journey, which might save money and, she has heard, offers less risk than Michael expects with snow ploughs now so active on approach roads. Michael jibs at the possibility of driving on chains, let alone trying to fix chains in a driving blizzard, and says it is better to book a hotel with an air package. Though some hotels are happy to bargain with the car tourer, especially in Italy and sometimes in Austria, it takes up valuable time and beginners have enough to worry about. Better to go for the package, he argues, with the benefit of a representative's advice for the little things they will not know. It is someone to turn to if there is trouble like stolen skis, which require deposi-

1. The fresher you are the softer you fall. Most beginners take spills as part of the fun.

2. Thisway thataway. Directions signs at St Moritz suggest some of the confusions in skiing. Everyone has an angle . . .

3. Swimming pool at Seefeld. Halfway across the pool at Alpe d'Huez, a much higher resort, I almost drowned as the effects of altitude hit me.

4. Ski toting is annoyingly difficult for a beginner. Rubber clips are easily lost. Tie the skis together with the safety straps, and carry them with the tips forward and the binding just behind the shoulder. For shorter distances, use them like a giant walking-stick.

5. Starting off at St Anton. At any level of ability, a composed start sets the tone for the entire run.

6. The snow plough. First base in orthodox ski instruction, but not with the Graduated Learning Method. Unless edged hard, the skis slide straight forward. Weighted one side or the other, the skier turns.

7. Ski Evolutif, or GLM. The learning method whereby skiers progress from short (1·3-metre) skis to longer ones as their technique and experience improve. Robert Blanc, founder of Ski Evolutif at Les Arcs, demonstrates the ski lengths.

8. The drag lift, otherwise known as the poma, button or soup plate. Beginners have to master these, even on the nursery slope. It's easy when you know how!

9. Over the bumps. Intermediate and advanced skiers come to enjoy their challenge, but beginners find them frightening at first.

10. Flaine's central meeting ground. Modern French resorts are built round the village green – except that it is white.

11. Reindeer on Cairngorm. In the Alps they would die for lack of sustenance. In northern Scotland, where 100 feet is the equivalent of 1000 feet in the Alps, the deer can feed on Arctic lichen. Scotland has at least given Britain a serious ski scene.

12. Hillend artificial slope in Edinburgh, the largest in Europe and an important part of the serious Scottish ski scene.

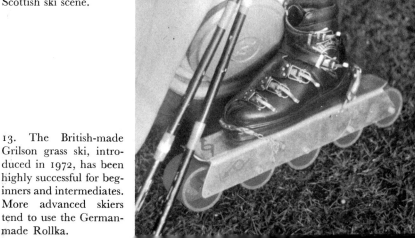

13. The British-made Grilson grass ski, introduced in 1972, has been highly successful for beginners and intermediates. More advanced skiers tend to use the German-made Rollka.

14. Cross-country style. Most Alpine ski resorts now have courses, or loipes, for this traditionally Nordic form of ski-ing. It is cheaper (no lifts to bother with), technically easier and safer.

tions at the local police station and argy-bargy with the hire shop. Jenny still hankers after taking a car, which she believes can save money and be useful at the resort. Hull to Zeebrugge or Harwich to the Hook of Holland on the overnight ferry can provide the early springboard for a nine to ten hour journey, principally on German autobahns, into Austria or Italy. Hoverlloyd also have an inclusive rate for drivers and passengers between Ramsgate and Calais in the low season. Whichever way they go, Michael reckons that they must budget on an overnight stop in each direction. The nearest French resort is about ten hours' driving, but mostly on toll motorways which can add over £20 to the costs. French petrol in 1977 was a third as much again as British.

Michael checks the car situation further. Although United Kingdom insurance is valid in the EEC countries and in Austria, Finland, Norway, Sweden and Switzerland, it covers only the legal bare minimum, and a green card from his own insurance company is necessary for the driver, passengers and car. This can cost as much again as the standard AA or RAC get-you-home service. Petrol must be computed at £1.25 a gallon (Italy provides tourist coupons with a twenty-four per cent discount, from motoring organisations or tourist offices or at the borders). Careful checks must be made of freezing levels of both engine water and windscreen solutions. Alpine villages, where a car is left out overnight, can be minus twenty degrees Centigrade, so double the usual amount of anti-freeze is needed. Michael is also advised by knowledgeable Alpine drivers that he should practise ice driving techniques on a skidpan, learning how to steer into a skid – as the rear wheels break right, you steer right, then swiftly over to the other lock before you overcorrect. AA and RAC schemes cover breakdown and vehicle recovery, but must be added to the cost of travel. Do-it-yourself also involves medical cover. With an overnight stop in both directions, Michael reasons that it would probably still be cheaper for the family man to go by car – though not if the children are too young to get out and push if they do have to stop on a tricky hill. The rule with snowy or icy going is for uphill traffic to keep moving wherever possible, engaging the highest gear possible for the conditions to avoid wheel spin. Michael also looks at fly-drive, with hire cars available at Genoa, Turin and Milan for a budget price.

In the end the size of their party decides them. Five is too many for a medium-sized saloon with all the baggage they have to carry – two are experienced skiers, taking their own skis. The other three will have too much on their plate as novice skiers for the extra worries of a car journey. Michael and Jenny keep it in mind for their second, third or fourth year.

Having opted for a package, what sort of package and with whom? They discover that Combined Services have some excellent arrangements, with only a nominal membership fee needed to become eligible, and although the number of resorts is restricted they are places like Zermatt, Davos, St Moritz, Wengen and Cervinia. The Ski Club of Great Britain (118 Eaton Place, London SW1; tel. 235 4711) not only has reduced package arrangements with chosen tour operators – the cash difference is not huge, but it all helps – but many resorts offer members ten per cent reductions for ski hire, lift passes or shop purchases. They also have weekend flights at reduced rates to Geneva (for France as well as Switzerland) and Zurich (for Switzerland and Austria). Other travel services offer return flights to Munich, Zurich and Geneva at less than half the regular fares with hostel accommodation – which may be used or not – included, but they require you to travel on specific days.

Membership of the SCGB offers many other services, including representatives at most leading resorts, an excellent magazine, *Ski Survey*, chock-a-block with information, a bar and restaurant in London, equipment and holiday advice, guided and unguided tours for all ages, ski proficiency tests, holidays for beginners and young people, and concessions in London and provincial shops ranging from furniture to cars. Membership (£9 a year in 1977) is the next move for Jenny and Michael if their first holiday is a success.

Jenny has heard that chalet and self-catering apartment holidays reduce expense and frequently bring together cheery bunches of people. Chalets can mean the hire of a two-person studio apartment in Saas Fee for about £40 a week or a nine-room villa in Gstaad with private heated swimming pool for over £500. Swiss Chalets, John Morgan and Supertravel (see page 214) all specialise in do-it-yourself chalets and flats, where resident reps get in the linen, in some cases make the beds, and put food and a bottle of wine ready for arrival. They explain all the foldaway arrangements and electrical ware, and are on hand for trouble, whether with lost hire equipment or language.

In effect this is a do-most-of-it-yourself holiday and I can recommend it, having sampled it in Val d'Isère with my family. We went by plane, but were still able to carry a number of provisions which were either expensive in themselves in a ski resort, or sold in awkwardly large quantities. Various things went wrong – as ever – but the memory was of a highly successful holiday. The most irritating was the theft of hired skis on the first day, Sunday. Moving day is vulnerable everywhere. In this instance the flat block provided only one key for the flatlet itself and for the individual ski cupboard in the hall. In the twenty minutes while I went to get the key, the family being in the flatlet, I was unwise enough to leave my skis in the hall. When I returned they had gone, and the fact that my children were on the balcony made no difference. At this point our operator's representative proved her resource, negotiating with both the hire shop and the police, and at least ensuring that the skis were quickly replaced with a minimum loss of ski-ing time. I had asked specifically for ski loss to be covered on my insurance and so was able to recover later the £60 demanded, but it meant the encashment of an additional £30 with a Barclaycard and cheque at a bank which accepted Carte Bleu identification. It is always advisable to have money in hand, or a credit card facility.

Chalets staffed by resident girls are a curiously English phenomenon, typically a product of the 'sixties, but as much part of the scene now as long-haired men or girls in jeans. Younger people seem to love the idea – one big, jolly party, complete strangers accepted as bosom friends on the instant, groups fading into other groups. At one time it was obviously based on South Ken and Earls Court flat styles and plenty of easy-come, easy-go relationships. Things seem to have matured now. Chalet operators and chalet girls have a well-polished routine. Whole hotels are now taken up for a season in some resorts, with English girls doing the catering and supervising, guests pouring their own drinks and logging them up, the whole thing going with an English party swing. Ages are more mixed these days, with the middle-aged also taking advantage of the cheaper rates. It is a style of holiday very much for English English, or for beginner groups wanting familiar things to lean on and unfamiliar things explained in familiar accents.

Michael and Jenny talk it over with their group. The two experienced skiers, Brian and Jean, want to absorb more of the atmosphere of a foreign country. Ann, the fifth member, has skied twice before but is open-minded. All agree they will be going to ski school, for much the same reasons although their standards are very different. They all want to improve their ski-ing, Michael and Jenny from scratch, Brian and Jean to ski consistent parallel turns, Ann to move from snowplough turns and stems to stem christies which will enable her to ski in more challenging country. Michael and Jenny listen to the ski terms and fix them in their minds without truly comprehending their meaning. All in good time.

Because of their varying requirements, they decide in the end on Austria, and Seefeld seems a resort which has something for each of them. It is reasonably close to Munich, the air terminal for most Austrian resorts, and it is busy and lively while retaining many of its ancient chalets and inns. There is cross-country ski-ing, just in case Michael or Jenny prove to be downhill ski-ing drop-outs, or their boots start to murder them. And the Seefelder Joch and Gschwandtkopf look to provide reasonable scope for the other three.

There are a few disadvantages to Seefeld compared with some other villages. Because of its popularity it is not the cheapest resort. It is on a sunny, south-facing shelf, but its snow record is not as good as that of, say Lech, which is in a natural snow bowl. It is also within reach of biggish German population centres and of Innsbruck itself, which means crowds at weekends when the snow reports are favourable. It is also on a railway line. But there are no perfect resorts. It has north-facing slopes where the snow is retained, and is well forested for further snow conservation. Jenny wants a lively, vital place and is prepared to put up with some of the consequences. If ski-ing fails, she argues, there is a swimming bath, skating rink, some good night spots and bars, shops, coffee and cake shops, and lots of people to see.

They decide on an ancient inn which has been enlarged and modernised upstairs, although, they are assured, keeping its simple wood-walled dining room and green baize door draught excluders. Beer is available vom fasch, or on draught, and the rooms have shower or bath. They consult a map of the village and see that the nursery slope is reasonably big for Jenny and Michael, and is within five to ten minutes walk of the hotel. Ski school and lift passes are available at a discount from the English tour operator, but the beginners are advised to leave the matter of lift passes until they are there. It is not worth their buying a season ticket for every run when they will only be capable of a small proportion of them, and will in any case be guided by their instructors.

They decide to book ski school through their tour operator, because they get a ten per cent reduction, having checked that it will involve two hours in the morning and two in the afternoon. Jenny is reluctant to commit the afternoon, wanting the opportunity to try things out on her own or simply to ice skate if she feels like it. Many ski schools now recognise this preference and have morning-only sessions. The others talk her out of it. 'You can never see yourself as a reasonable instructor will see you,' says Brian. 'You just carry on doing the same old things badly or wrongly, losing your confidence and enthusiasm. We might help you for a bit but you'll feel guilty about taking up our ski-ing time. You won't have the advantage of a group thing, of being a bit competitive with each other, getting a bit of a kick when you do something better than the fellow who looks so athletic. Having a laugh when he falls over. Then when you do, too!' Brian likes the discipline and challenge of an advanced class, but he also believes that the fear factor in ski-ing is best controlled when you are in a group and others help to relieve your feelings either by achieving something or by failing. He trusts, too, the ski school instructor's knowledge of his own mountains and of the most interesting ways down them. In the end, Jenny's residual dislike of anything smacking of school is overborne. Ski school it will be.

Chapter 5

Getting Ready

Boots, skis and sticks can be hired in Britain with major savings and with more time and care from a shop where you can readily communicate. Against this is the burden of transporting them and perhaps embarrassment at carrying equipment you barely know how to use. Equipment can also be pre-booked by the tour operators, at a discount, which has the advantage that it can be changed or adjusted readily at the hirer's shop. But I have never known any objections from continental ski shops when I have presented personal equipment for repair or adjustment – they get it all the time from their own nationals – providing you pick your time and go in the middle of the morning or afternoon.

Except for Italian equipment bought in Italy, prices in Britain will be notably cheaper than in a ski resort, where shops want a maximum mark-up from a captive public. Moreover British shops usually sell off previous season's stock at a considerable discount in the autumn and spring, and excellent bargains are to be had in boots, skis, goggles and clothes, with reductions sometimes of thirty per cent and more. This is certainly the time to buy for more experienced skiers who recognise what is a good basic product irrespective of the season's fashions. The shopkeepers are on the receiving end of the modish ski market in the need to clear stock, but you cannot be too sorry for them – the mark-ups take it all into account.

CLOTHING

Jenny has an anorak she wears for Saturday morning shopping, but Brian says it will not do. It is not padded on the shoulders, where knobbly ski bindings have to nestle. Most modern ski anoraks just button across the Adam's apple; anorak material directly against the skin is cold and unpleasant in sub-zero temperatures, so you get little advantage from the collar. The front should also have a fly to prevent wind whistling through the holes of the zip, and to stop the zip rubbing coldly against the face when you are sitting hunched up on a chair lift. A substantial lining is essential. Finnish-made anoraks available at some British departmental stores are excellent value. They are at least designed for cold weather and, in most cases, for the possibility of ski-ing. Some from Hong Kong are excellent, others are windcheaters for temperate climates. Jenny's anorak has a hood tucking into the back lining, but it has no elasticated lining fitting tightly against the wrist, so a fall may mean a sleeve full of cold wet snow. Finally, it has only two vertical pockets; although these are zipped, they will be inadequate for the things Jenny may want to carry – handkerchief, purse or wallet, ski pass or tickets, sun glasses, ski strap or rubber for keeping the skis together when she is carrying them, sun cream, lip salve, comb, maybe cigarettes and lighter and, for a girl, make-up. Four external, horizontal or slanting pockets – it is too easy to drop something into the snow from a vertical opening – and inside pockets are desirable unless you want to wear a strap round the waist with a banana-shaped bag at the back. Skiers know them as bum bags. For the sake of figure-hugging fashion, some skiers of both sexes give up pocket space, but it can be highly inconvenient. A pocket with a 'window' for ski lift passes is a valuable accessory.

Jenny likes the look of the dungarees, known sometimes as salopettes, and matching shortie anorak, and thinks she might wear one or both as casual wear at home if she chooses wisely. She decides this will be a credit card extravagance. Michael gets a Finnish-made anorak at a large departmental store for £15 and is well pleased. It has most of the desirable features, and is in a non-slip material of sensible colour. He does not want to wear anything flash – psychedelic orange and pink, or striped trousers – in case he turns out to be a ski-ing duffer. Women, and more confident males, enjoy the chance to sport plenty of colour – it is what the game is about for a great many.

Trousers or salopettes? It is a matter of style and practicality. Jenny laughed herself silly at Michael in blue dungarees, but there are many colour combinations which flatter a good figure, male or female, they keep out snow in a fall and are generally warmer. It is usual to buy them with matching jackets which tend to be shorter than the conventional anorak covering the bottom. The salopette should be lined and possibly quilted on the inside, and have snow traps inside the legs to stop snow squirting up. In the end, Michael hires from a specialist ski-shop a pair of nearly new trousers with a small amount of flare covering the top clips, and a snow-trap lining. He crouches down a few times to ensure the crutch seam will not part with his first schuss, a cold and possibly embarrassing experience. Trousers like this are worn over the socks, usually with a wide looped piece under the instep to hold them fairly taut. Trousers tucking inside the boot have gone out of fashion – ribbed seams were just another way of bruising the ankle.

At a sale, Brian buys a short-look jacket and matching salopette for £40 and is well satisfied. It is a little known manufacturer but wiser British retailers hunt them down at the international shows.

Ski outfitting is still a little trappy. An expensive item may not be the best designed for the job, only the best looking. Most stretch trousers now are a mixture of artificial fibre (terylene, polyester, nylon etc). One pair I bought lost its windproof qualities after the first dry clean. They were still all right provided I wore woollen long johns underneath, but these I wear whatever the quality of trousers (it is cheaper still to wear pyjama trousers). Ideally trousers should have a wool element as it is much warmer than almost any artificial fibre. The snag is that wool tends to pill round the stiffer fibres, particularly where you sit yourself on soup plates and T-bars. Jenny will be advised to take a couple of pairs of thicker denier tights. Novice skiers take too little account of wind cold – the consequence of their own speed (yes, even a learner) in an exposed place at higher altitudes. They also have more hanging around, either watching or recovering breath. I have found a pair of over-trousers necessary from time to time. These are padded nylon and cover my legs rather like cowboy chaps, with a rather tricky double zip arrangement on each of the outer sides. They are available in a variety of thicknesses. Michael buys a single pair of heavy nylon long johns (they dry out overnight), reasoning that warmth is a good invest-ment for muscular exercise of any kind. The key to ski clothing is a measure of adjustability to different con-ditions and body temperatures. It is easier to take off than put on. The weather as you open your hotel window in the morning may not be the same at 6000 feet in the afternoon, so go prepared.

Knowing about cold is important for all grades of skier. Mountain air is much drier than the moist, basically sea air commonly experienced in a British winter. Damp conducts heat quickly. Body heat is very soon lost in British conditions where a degree or two above zero feels much colder than ten degrees below in the Alps. British snow, often containing salt particles, is much wetter than Alpine snow. Falling over on Cairngorm is a wetter business than falling over in Zermatt, St Anton or Megève. Mitts or gloves not made for the job quickly become soaked. Care is always needed not to go on ski-ing if the hand is going numb with wet cold. Snow inside a glove will quickly cause frostbite unless it is cleared out.

SKIS

Recent years have seen two major ski revolutions – the switch to shorter skis and to hard-shell boots. The chief effect has been a major speeding up in the time a beginner takes to become proficient. Ski learning methods have had a drastic shake-up, and many traditional areas of Europe are still struggling in the wake of change. Learning by the short-ski method – GLM or ATM (American Teaching Method) in the USA, Ski Evolutif in France – is one of the effects. What made it possible, however, was the successful exploitation of modern synthetic materials, both in skis and boots, in a hungry market.

The problem now is to choose among so many clamouring alternatives. In skis and boots, as in clothes, it is hard to distinguish between what is fashionable and what is enduring. The market is aimed primarily at the regular skier who will wear out his skis and boots in about two to three seasons. Those with regular access to Scottish centres come into this category. Ski-ing in Scotland can be like low tide at Brighton, OK for the soles if you pick your path through the pebbles. Anyone who skis hard and ruthlessly there will wear out a conventional pair of skis in a season. The sensible choose a ski priced according to their ability. What is certain is that British prices will be lower than foreign because our tariff barriers are less. The quality of ski is usually in ratio to price; the better you are the more you pay.

While Jenny and Michael will be hiring their skis at the resort, it helps to know enough to avoid being foisted off with bad or poorly maintained skis. Brian needs to buy new skis, and they join him in the hope of picking up some tips. Brian was lucky enough to sell off his five-year-old skis of 205 centimetres – or 6 ft 8 in – to a man of fifteen stone who believed he still needed that length for stability. In fact he was a skier who had learned a steered-turn technique in the 'fifties and was reluctant even to try and adapt his technique to a shorter ski.

But how short is short, Jenny asks, and, as so often, the innocent question goes to the heart of a problem. Such confusion existed a little while ago that representatives of two rival London ski retailers, Michael Evans of Pindisports and Martin Grace of Lillywhites, produced a paper, 'Short or Shorter Skis', combining their own experience with that of the British Director of Ski Coaching, John Shedden, Peter Forbes, equipment adviser to the Ski Club of Great Britain, Douglas Godlington, editor of the British Ski Instructors' manual, and Sandy Tebbutt, chairman of the English Ski Committee and a ski retailer. At the end of 1976 their conclusions were proved right. Sales of short skis jumped from twenty per cent in 1974 to seventy-five per cent, partly due, no doubt, to their personal influence, partly because word of mouth supported what might otherwise be a sales device. The short ski did make learning quicker and easier; it did improve the performance of the mature skier; it did enable people to turn under more control; there was no great sacrifice in speed to all except the young, aggressive skier with good technique.

Grace and Evans used tables from the French ski manufacturer, Rossignol, giving best lengths of ski for two basic grades of skier, the good to expert and the beginner-intermediate. They gave the comparative lengths of standard and short skis for specific height and weight. Brian, who is 34, 5 ft 10 ins and 12 stone, can parallel turn and is thus in the good to expert class. He quickly sees that the ideal standard length ski for him is 200 to 207 cms, and his equivalent shortie 175 to 195. Jenny, who is 8 stone 10 lbs and 5 ft 5 ins, sees that her standard length is 180 to 185 and her shortie 160 to 170. There is a further grade of skier, the freestyler or hot-dogger, who since he is capable of a complete somersault on skis needs to be pretty expert. He will prefer a ski around 185 centimetres long, while another free expression skier, the ballet man or woman, will prefer 150 to 170.

As a rule of thumb for the novice, intermediate, or less aggressive skier, head height is now about right for Compacts. The youngster, say between sixteen and twenty-one, who is fit and athletic, can go for a ski three inches above his or her height. The novices of this age are likely to learn quickly, and after a couple of fourteen-day holidays will be seeking to ski fast. The standard ski will suit them best from the start. Confusion over short ski definitions principally came about because many failed to understand the difference in design between a standard ski and a short ski. The true short ski, best known as the Compact, is made to carry a skier of specific weight at a slower speed than the standard ski. It is wider, although only by about six millimetres or a quarter of an inch.

Skis have a romantic history. They are complex and beautiful precision instruments. A millimetre here is not a millimetre there. The rate of bankruptcy among ski manufacturers is extraordinary. Men become infatuated with their designs or their belief in certain materials, and business sense may fly out of the window. The ski, to them, is a kind of mistress. The 2,500-year-old Ovrebo ski in the ski museum of the Holmenkollen, Oslo, is a simple board. Technology led the ski maker into combinations of material which capitalized on the advantages of each other. The solid hickory mountain touring ski of 1928 was succeeded in the 1930s by the splitkein, with thin layers of different wood glued together on the plywood principle for a stronger and more resilient ski. The splitkein might be layered not only like a sandwich but like a neapolitan ice-cream, side by side. They came so heavy to the US Army's Tenth Mountain Division that Nick Hock, publisher of *Ski Magazine*, recalls, 'You could ski for two weeks in powder snow without seeing your skis. They were like submarines.'

America took the next major step forward with Harry and Hart Holmberg introducing the first metal ski, called the Hart, in 1955, but a year later Toni Sailer of Austria became the first Alpine skier ever to win three Olympic gold medals on a Kästle wood ski. Kästle's advance was to use a less expensive ash core which produced a livelier slalom ski. Howard Head, a Martin aircraft engineer who could not ski, when asked to design for someone who could, started with the premise that a heavily stressed structure made of wood was absurd. Living in penury for eight years, he came up with a ski built to an I-beam principle with the top and bottom 'skins' connected by a core. The Head Standard that emerged changed the nature of ski construction for all time. It had an aluminium top and bottom, plastic sides and a core of sandwiched plywood layers set on edge. It had one-piece steel edges which took part of the strain of the ski. Moreover it did not have to be hand-made. It was a typically American, production-line job, and it helped bring easier ski-ing within range of a mass public for the first time. The Head needed no special care, it did not warp, and broke only under severe stress. It was three times as flexible at its tips as a wood ski, it turned like a dream in soft snow; in fact it turned with wonderful ease in any snow. It was affectionally called the 'Cheater', so many were its advantages over wood. Its one great drawback, however, made it a failure as a racing ski. Metal vibrates rapidly, and it jumped around at speed. Head introduced rubber as a damper, but resisted glass fibre.

Far away in Kufstein, Austria, on the German border, Franz Kneissl, heir to a coach and wheel factory that started making splitkeins in 1936, was putting all his money on a fibreglass casing and a young racer called Karl Schranz. For the White Star ski which was to succeed the Head as a worldwide best seller, Kneissl retained his loyal Tyrolean wood craftsmen for wood lamination underneath the casing. Largely because of the money he made from Kneissl, Schranz was disqualified from the 1972 Sapporo Olympics. The son of a tunnel worker dying prematurely from disease of his smoke-wracked lungs, Schranz, through the White Star, became an Austrian national hero cheered through the streets by a quarter of a million people on his return from Sapporo. Kneissel next introduced a foam core and sentiment had to disappear. Today there are no woodworkers left at Kufstein, only foam and fibreglass moulders.

Glass fibre is a compound, a mat of fine strands with polyester or epoxy resin hardening around the fibres.

Where Kneissel used glass fibre in sheets, Dynamic, the French ski maker, employed wet-wrap, a more complicated process with the glass fibre wrapped around the core while still wet, rather like the mummy process, giving different properties to the ski over its length. Thus a soft tip and hard tail in the VR-17 helped the Grenoble University ski professor, George Joubert, confirm his avalement ski technique theories and Jean-Claude Killy personify them. With the skier leaning forward, the ski would carve a strict route through snow with no time-wasting skid. Out of corners he could sit back more, the ski accelerating or jetting forward. Dynamic introduced the first plastic base, which started the process whereby waxing of Alpine skis was eliminated, and the 'cracked edge' theory, whereby set-in edges with hairline cracks would assist the flexing of the ski. It was the perfect instrument of its time, but with such innovation and processing it was never a cheap ski.

Rossignol, another French firm, began when Abel Rossignol, owner of a spindle factory in the Isère valley, was smitten with a pair of skis acquired on a trip to Norway. With Emile Allais he helped design a laminate ski which gained Allais the world championship in 1937, an Olympic victory for Henri Oreiller in 1948, and a world championship for Christian Pravda in 1954. At the 1960 Squaw Valley Olympics the Allais Major made the all-metal racing breakthrough which had eluded Head, the French racer, Jean Vuarnet, making best use of its properties by the introduction of l'oeuf, or the super-streamlined egg position, in downhill racing.

It was a subsequent ski, the Strato, which founded Rossignol's fortune as one of the world's major manufacturers and a big rival to the Austrian manufacturers, Fischer, Kneissl, Blizzard and Atomic, especially in the lucrative markets of North America. The Strato used a glass fibre sandwich but had a gentler action than the Dynamic. It was suitable for women racers and for holiday skiers, so the Canadian Nancy Greene's giant slalom gold medal on it at Grenoble in 1968 was especially important publicity. Ski manufacturers have never had any illusions about the value of racing success and endorsement. The rise of Atomic skis in the 1970s was almost entirely due to the success of the Austrian girl, Annemarie Proell.

Hot dog, or freestyle ski-ing, has accelerated the move into short skis. Balletic, bumps and acrobatic forms require a ski no longer than 185 centimetres, and a new set of names, for example Wayne Wong and Suzy Chaffee, a moderate racer formerly, well publicised by ABC Television, have boosted the process in the USA. Finally, the spread of the short-ski method in America and France, has left many graduates of the system content to buy at the length they finished off in school – 160 centimetres.

Seventy per cent of the skis on display at recent international ski shows have been Compacts, and ski schools throughout Europe have come to accept them, albeit with reluctance or qualification in traditionalist centres. Their construction remains basically of two types, sandwich and torsion box, as with the standard ski, and characteristics vary according to weighting, shaping and the materials used. The cores may be of wood, foam (mostly polyurethane or acrylic), aluminium honeycomb, or a combination of each. The first material Howard Head tried when he began building experimental skis was aluminium honeycomb, which is widely used in jet aircraft to carry heavy structural loads. Until recently the ski industry could not find a honeycomb that did not come apart, but two American ski-makers, Hart and Century, have overcome the problem. The sandwich or box outside the core may be of aluminium alloy, plastic, glass fibre reinforced plastic or rubber. The sandwich design must have good bonding properties. The box skis, which are made individually, unlike the sandwich, must be closely matched in weight, stiffness, flex and balance.

P-Tex is widely used for the soles, giving a durable surface which nevertheless suffers gouges affecting performance. They are readily filled in with an aerosol or candle wax. The groove running along the sole helps keep a straight track, rather like a tyre tread. One innovation in 1977 was to eliminate the groove in the section under the boot to help the swivelling motion. The shape of a ski, as much as its construction materials, affects its use and performance, but these Jenny can think about when she is about to go on the snow.

BINDINGS

Brian sold his old bindings with the skis, so he has the additional expense of a new set of bindings which he is determined will give him the most up-to-date knowledge and workmanship available. Bindings are the clip devices which attach a skier's boot to the ski. They are designed to hold him rigidly to the ski through all the stresses of normal ski-ing, but release him in a fall before the leverage of the ski can do him injury. A modern binding has built-in elasticity which allows small, momentary movements of the boot at higher speed and returns it to centre. When the twisting forces become sustained the binding releases. Whether cheap or expensive, no binding is safe unless it is properly set. Ignorance, laziness or an assumption of someone else's expertise, which can be widely misplaced at a busy ski-hire shop, lead to accidents and badly torn tendons, muscles and cartilages or, rather less often these days, broken legs.

The level of British or American accidents on the

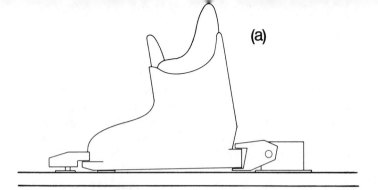

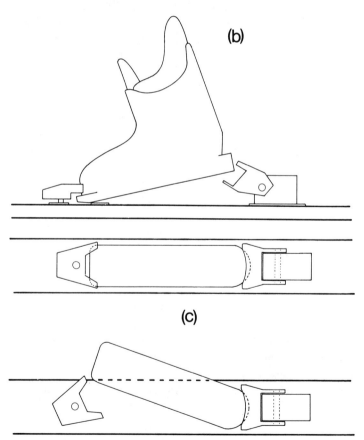

Fig. 5 Bindings. (a) Step-in heel unit before release. (b) Step-in heel unit after release during a forward fall. (c) The action of the toe binding before and after release during a sideways twisting fall.

Continent is much higher than the native, principally because the fortnight-a-year man is rarely as fit. There is also a psychological aspect. Learner skiers tend to think they should fall, so fall they do. The Swiss, Austrian, Italian or Frenchman living in or close to a ski village does not think in this way. They do update their equipment regularly and generally care for it. They tend not to ski in bad conditions, where Britons and Americans may ski trying to get their holiday money's worth. Even so, all accident rates are down in recent years because of big strides in binding design and, as far as Britons are concerned, growing expertise in home ski shops where equipment is bought or hired and knowledge passed on by an increasing core of BASI instructors.

Leading makes such as Ess, Geze, Look, Marker, Salomon and Tyrolia offer a range of bindings suited to ability, while Gertsch and imitators have a plate binding of a different basic design. An aggressive, expert sixteen-stone skier will need binding adjustments able to take heavier stresses than a seven-stone woman beginner. His fear will be premature release. It is hardly that of the beginner to intermediate although, at the other extreme, constant stepping out of a binding is highly irritating. This applies especially in soft snow, which at once cakes under the boots. Cleaning it off with cold, scrabbling fingers, or poking away with the ski stick while trying to balance on one foot, is a beginner's nightmare. Unless the snow is removed the ski welt does not slide firmly under the clips. In that event you may be out again at the next turn, which wrecks concentration and confidence. Then there is risk of over-tightening the binding through ignorant fiddling, so that it does not open for the slow fall which a novice is most likely to suffer.

Skiers who do not exceed twenty mph tend to have their bindings set unnecessarily high. The loosest adjustment holding a skier to his ski for his particular style is the safest setting. Most bindings have separate adjustments for boot length, height of the heel, height of the toe, correct forward pressure between heel and toe, and finally for release – right and left at the toe to cope with sideways falls, and upwards at the heel for forward falls. Some bindings also release upwards at the toe and sideways at the heel. Gertsch are of a different type, with the boot attached to a plate which releases backwards, forwards or sideways. The more release angles there are, the more the opportunity for inadvertent release, which is another reason for constantly checking the adjustment. Gertsch are favoured by many hiring institutions, especially British artificial slopes, where boot and plate go together for children and others with no equipment of their own. The accident rate here is notably low, which must be a point in their favour, although speeds are low. They are also good where a boot is wearing on the sole or welt, though it is an unwise skier who skis with a sole starting to bend.

Brian, as an experienced skier, must make a sophisticated choice. The strongest-setting Salomon available to the public in 1977 was the 555 Equipe requiring a minimum force of 173 lbs to make the binding release at the heel. A men's competition binding requires 264 lbs. It is for the downhiller capable of over 100 mph, who may hit a compression (a level area after a downhill section) with a terrible forward jerk. They are bindings suited to skiers applying sudden shock rather than gradually increasing pressure. I had a damaging fall on a 555 because I was not heavy enough for the setting, was not ski-ing fast enough and did not fall hard enough. In addition the pressure was exactly forwards, without sideways effect of any kind. The Teflon anti-friction pad on the sole of the ski is designed to reduce the clamping effect of friction between sole and ski when the weight is abruptly thrown forward. Given the slightest chance it helps to cause a sideways slide out of the ski. Mechanical devices such as the Tyrolia Rolldisc or Cubco Swinger serve the purpose better than a pad, though they need mild maintenance. Now the Gertsch patent has been broken the plate binding will probably be more widely used everywhere.

Choice of binding comes down to weight, bone strength and ability, best expressed by beginner, average or expert. The shop may be able to measure the head of the tibia to check whether the bones are smaller or larger than normal for weight, though this cannot be foolproof since different bones have different qualities. Some bones have holes like pinheads, others like split peas. Everyone knows about brittle-boned sportsmen, and this does not depend on size. But the shop will be doing what it can, and there are safety standard tables which help. The skier ought then to answer honestly whether he is an aggressive skier or not – two skiers of the same weight and ability will ski in totally different ways, one with plenty of shock, the other more smoothly. On this advice the shop will be able to recommend a binding and setting. Manufacturers' instructions are usually very clear, so verbally and on paper the skier ought to be in no doubt.

Binding testing machines are not infallible, for not only is there the problem of bone density; there can be faulty readings, and in particular room temperatures soften up the boot compared to sub-zero mountain conditions. Not every manufacturer recommends a testing machine. Salomon give tables based on production line checks from which settings may be made unless the boot is non-standard. Modern bindings, however, are made for modern boots – a deformed boot is a danger. And all require checking every day for correct setting and opening pressures.

Brian in the end settles for a Compact ski of 185 centimetres. Although a good skier he is not in any sense a 'bomber'. He would rather take a steep slope comfortably, turning under control, than ski close to his limits. He chooses a binding with a minimum release force in the second division, so to speak, of the manufacturers' classification, and incorporating a ski stopper. This is a recent device taking the place of safety straps. Jenny was under a false impression about safety straps. She thought that in some way they helped prevent falls. They are simply short retaining straps, usually elasticated, fastened to the heel piece of the binding and clipping around the lower leg. When the ski comes off in a fall the strap will prevent the ski accelerating down the mountainside and possibly piercing someone like a spear. There is always a danger with a learner that if a ski comes off repeatedly he will not, in a moment of distraction, reclip the safety strap. The ski stopper is a sprung metal shoe under the ski boot. If the boot releases the pressure as in a fall, the shoe digs two prongs into the snow, thus preventing the ski skidding away. A ski spinning on a safety strap can give a falling skier a nasty clout. The ski stopper eliminates this, but the ski may be left awkward distances away or even disappear in a bank of soft snow.

Few people can ski satisfactorily on one ski, and to try and get down a slope on foot poses impossible problems when you sink in up to the thigh. It happened to me once, half an hour before dark, when heavy snowfall had obliterated the piste. The lights of Andermatt were already carpeting the valley, and a night on the Gemstock in those conditions would have tested my survival capacity severely. Fortunately the last few runners in a British championship were still ski-ing, and they came to my rescue. One shouldered my hired skis – a binding on one had broken – and waited as I floundered in the deep snow. A young Scots girl, skidding to a halt, had the best answer. 'Bum it,' she shouted, which meant choosing the steepest slope away from the run, the markers of which were almost indiscernible in the thick snow and failing light, and pushing off toboggan-style on my bottom. It worked for long enough to get onto more packed snow about 500 feet down. Then I used my ski sticks to take longish, running strides with my weight never poised long enough for my feet to sink in deeply. Fortunately the snow had stopped and visibility was just about good enough to pick a path. It was dodgy, but it worked. Twilight had become near darkness by the bottom of the run, where an elderly couple, a doctor and his wife, members of the White Hare Ski Club, still waited with an urn of hot Ovaltine for anyone arriving late or in difficulty. They were never so welcome. Even as we chatted, two piste workers employed by the local tourist office skied out of the darkness of the mountain, one holding up a circular cable from one of my ski bindings like a jackdaw with a ring. It was comforting to know that there was such vigilance.

The cable was part of an old Kandahar binding, in general Alpine use in the 1960s but superseded by the step-in binding. Kandahar are still widely used in Norway, since they are adjustable for touring ski-ing, where the heel is lifted from a lightweight ski for easier and faster passage over undulating surfaces. Adjustment of the cable under clips at the heel clamps the boot firmly to the heel for downhill only. A few middle-aged to elderly skiers still use them.

BOOTS

For the most part the British, too, seem to have clung

on longest to leather boots. They ski only for a limited period, leather is traditionally a quality material where plastic is not, and it is more comfortable for walking. But this is dangerous reasoning. The many who want to return to ski-ing after a longish gap should throw their old boots into the waste bin. Even at a jumble sale they would be dangerous. The revolution in boot design has also revolutionised technique. Georges Joubert believes that boots have had a more significant effect on technique in the 'seventies even than skis. It is the main reason why Jenny and Michael will buy rather than hire for their holiday, though taking advantage of the hire-buy arrangement by which they can take them back and pay only the hire charge if the boots are unsuitable. A limited number of shops offer this service and Brian strongly recommends it. Unless the boots truly fit, the holiday, indeed their entire enthusiasm for ski-ing, may be forfeit. Fortunately this is well understood in most specialist shops, where advice and patience is likely to be readily offered (See Appendix 4). If it is not, you get up and go.

Different abilities, foot lengths and widths, and heights of instep, mean that boots should never be lumped into a package and sold with skis and bindings. A boot has three main characteristics: flexibility, height and fit. All depend on the way a skier skis and his weight and strength. A cautious lightweight needs the softest boot he can get, short of leather, which does not relate to the 'give' properties of a modern elasticated binding and so may release prematurely or not at all. A better skier is likely to be happier with a more rigid shell, and here the materials used in the construction are important. Principally they are thermoplastic, polyurethane, and adiprene. Thermoplastic is relatively light and soft, and likely to be preferred by beginners and by skiers with techniques wedded to leather boots. It is unlikely to stand as much hard wear as polyurethene, but it is cheaper and more comfortable. Polyurethene is a much heavier material, with more rigid properties for the aggressive skier, and lasts longer. Adiprene is polyurethene-based but lighter and a little more flexible. Like polyurethene, it has better insulating characteristics than thermoplastic, and will be rather warmer.

Many boots now have a detachable inner lining of Flofit, or a similar trade-named substance which, like putty or plasticine, gives to the configuration of foot and ankle. Feet swell according to muscular effort, with altitude also encouraging it. Less than a millimetre of swelling means skinning and bruising of the thin, vulnerable skin layers over shin and ankle, and then the boots start giving hell. The other trap is buying big boots which ride and chafe. In this case it is in the village, walking to and from the ski lift, rather than on the slopes, that the worst pain usually develops. Flofit is the best answer so far for what are basically contradictory requirements. Foam injection, an earlier development, undertaken with the skier standing in the boots, was a failure for three main reasons. Shop conditions were not those of the higher slopes, assistants were not always thorough enough and there was no subsequent 'give' for different foot conditions. Another radical alternative is the air boot, with an inner boot forming itself round the foot like a bladder. A small air pump and pressure gauge in theory enable the skier to adjust the bladder according to need. The higher you go the more air you let out. Flofit or its equivalent at present dominates the market, but there are snags. Skiers who leave their boots in the car boot in sub-zero temperatures ask for trouble. The Flo goes concrete hard in the mould of a skier finishing his day – hot and a bit swollen. They are instruments of torture until warmed up again, preferably by standing them close to a radiator for about an hour. No-one can pretend that enough of the problems have been solved. According to one manufacturer, the boot of the future will be all-purpose, with easily portable attachments for its role as a ski boot.

The height of the boot became an emotive subject in the early days of the rigid shell, when manufacturers were hard-selling a boot coming high up the leg to meet what was primarily a racing rather than a recreational need. Advanced skiers would appear to sit back when they used the jet or avalement technique, and support high on the calf muscles was helpful. This was confusing for the recreational skier, who had neither the quality of technique nor strength of thigh to do it this way, and would most often sit straight down on his bottom if he tried. Moreover the very high boots were especially uncomfortable when walking. Racers are plentifully endowed with transport and skivvies waiting on their attendance, recreational skiers are not. Effectively, however, it was the Swiss downhill team who revolted against stovepipe boots, hacking them down with those formidable all-purpose knives, and stopping the worst excesses. The Swiss maintained that the shin-crunchers cost them feel for snow and terrain, and boots of more sensible heights were adopted without serious loss of the edge control which rigid shell boots gave.

Today's boot must be comfortable. Highbacks are now flared for better fit at the calf, boot shafts are narrower for greater lateral support and edge control, the shells are canted forward, but not absurdly so, foot beds are contoured, and tongues and grips round the calf are better padded. Most makers have a boot top swivelling forward on a hinge under certain pressures. Others have an apparent hinge, but it is merely an articulation to allow forward flex which will not crunch the shin.

Good fit, the third of the imperatives, is still primarily the responsibility of the wearer. For example, Continental bootmakers have only the haziest idea of equivalent British sizing, so the figure on the boot can be safely ignored! A good assistant measures the foot and directly interprets it. The better boots are now articulated behind the ankle so that the top of the boot can 'give' with forward leg movement while still able to transmit essential pressures onto the ski or, equally, to ease them quickly. The Flofit lining ought to grip a little tight in the shop. It is made of latex and either cork or polystyrene to give it bulk. It compacts a little after a few days' wear, hence the need for a modicum of tightness; more boots are brought back because they are too big than too small.

In buying their boots, Michael and Jenny wear thick socks – looped wool outsides, smooth inners – and are determined to give themselves time. The boots will have to last for at least five years, and they do not want to buy the first thing that appears moderately right without trying at least three makes and possibly several shops. In the normal ski position, with knees a little forward, there should be no pressure on the toes. If you stand bolt upright and cannot feel the end of the boot it may be too big. There are four or five clips, though modern designs are attempting to reduce moving parts to a minimum and up-market there are rear-entry boots with only one or two clips. In trying on the multi-clip boot it is best to clip up at the bottom and work upwards, then tighten again in the same order.

The orthodox boot will have an overlap on the instep, and it surprises dealers how often people distort the shells by clipping up with the underlay crossed with the overlay. Jenny and Michael test for toe pressures, then push forward with the knees and watch for any tendency for the heel to lift upwards. Heel lift means less control of the skis. They press forward against the shinbones to see if there is obvious discomfort or untoward bulging, which means the boots are too wide; Jenny is aware that leading makers provide women's boots with narrower fittings. Does the boot flex as the leg goes forward? If not it is too stiff. Height is not the main consideration in itself since modern boots avoid the worst excesses and in any case are styled for flexibility. Having decided on a favourite pair, and compared price with price, Jenny and Michael walk around the shop for a good ten minutes to ensure that there are no pressure points. It is a bit of a pantomime, but worth it.

Brian has one more inquiry. Does he need wedges? Several British shops acquired canting machines from the USA after the case for wedging had been propounded by Warren Witherell in *How the Racers Ski*, an American book extensively quoted by the *Sunday Times* book, *We Learned to Ski*. Briefly, wedging means the insertion of tapered strips of plastic or metal between binding and ski to ensure that a bow-legged or knock-kneed skier stands flat on his skis. Charles Palmer, president of the International Judo Federation, whose sport had left him somewhat bandy, wrote a glowing testimonial to canting ('I have never enjoyed my ski-ing so much') in the Ski Club magazine. Michael Evans, of Pindisports, London, commented after a season of use that over-wedging was more disastrous than no wedging at all, and that although accurate machine readings below two degrees of differential were extremely difficult, many people felt that their money was well spent (at that time £5 for one ski, £9.50 for two). Martin Grace, of Lillywhites, found there was no great call for his machine and, although people with more acute conditions seemed much helped, was sceptical of its assistance to the great majority with only minor variations. 'You cannot make an unathletic person athletic through wedging,' he said. Brian examines the line from the inside of his knee cap to his ankle and decides it is straight enough not to worry.

GLOVES, HATS AND GOGGLES

Mittens are relatively cheap and effective, but they must be non-porous and big enough so that woollen gloves can be worn underneath. I have always favoured silicone-proofed leather gloves with reinforced pressure points and a good fleecy lining because I prefer the use of my fingers in carrying skis, showing a lift pass, adjusting snow goggles or any one of the major or minor needs. They are expensive, best bought in a British specialist shop, and you look after them. Thin nylon inner gloves add enormously to protection from cold.

Often I have skied without a hat, knowing I had a hood built into my anorak if the snow really came down or my ears started to get really cold. But most people look pretty silly in the little hoods normally stuffed into the lining of anoraks and, since it is a fashion sport, headgear matters. Every Alpine and Nordic nation has its traditional style. Norwegians have a tassled pom-pom, French, Austrians and Swiss variously shaped hats which give an engagingly different effect. French instructors at one time favoured white caps with ear pieces which made them look like Bleriot aviators. It is all part of the fun. Ski-ing is a bit of a show-off sport, and you buy your hat entirely as fancy takes you.

Goggles are the sort of extra a novice wonders if he can do without. The answer is no, for he cannot count on being lucky with the weather. They are primarily used in bad light and snow, when even a modest speed makes visibility difficult, and for glare. Snow driving hard into the eyes is a most disconcerting and disorientating experience, and after the first week the beginner could well find himself halfway up the mountain and badly in need of protection. He needs either good-quality wraparound plastic glasses with changeable yellow or smoke lenses – my own preference – or purpose-made goggles with foam liners, vents which help prevent misting up and, again, convertible lenses. Goggles can be pushed up over the hat when not needed, or doubled up round the arm of an anorak, but they are all too easily lost there. When you need them most, in a snow storm, they most readily mist up, and tips like smearing them with washing-up liquid are all the more aggravating for their impractibility in so many circumstances. The French-made glasses I use – bought for about £1.50 at the top of the Chanterella funicular at St Moritz – are easy to use, relatively scratch-free, double as sun glasses, and can be carried in a simple plastic case in an anorak pocket.

Protection from snow blindness is equally important. Eyes can become extremely sore from the combination of strong sunshine reflecting off almost unbroken snow. Some people are more vulnerable than others, and there is nothing worse than perfect weather spoiled by unwonted discomfort. Sun glasses of some description are a must. So is a small bottle of a soothing lotion such as Mureen. I also take a lipseal and remember to use it each day religiously, having several times suffered cold sores from wind and altitude exposure. The ultraviolet rays on a mountainside, in combination with wind or without, demand a high-quality sun cream which will keep radiation to a minimum. Ultraviolet rays are of two types: 'A' rays which are beneficial and tanning, and 'B' rays, in the shorter wavebands, which can cause sunburn and skin irritation. They do so whether the sun is in or out. A cream needs to keep out the 'B' and let in the 'A', and also be effective against wind chapping.

Uvistat, Bergasol, Piz Buin, Juventa, Uvex, Ambre Soleil and Bonne Belle all have excellent products for mountain use. It is as well, also, to take a balm just in case of accidental sunburn. Simple calomine cream is as good as any, though Jenny will want a gentler, less caky lotion.

PRE-SKI EXERCISES

Only the most naive of skiers takes off for the snow without some physical preparation. Getting fit to ski is much wiser than ski-ing to get fit. Children and students doing plenty of varied physical exercises as part of a learning curriculum may be just about exempt from the need. But I found on my first ski-ing holidays that even regular adult exercise – a weekly soccer match in winter, regular cricket, swimming and tennis in summer – were inadequate for the special demands of ski-ing. But what is an adequate and reasonable programme for men and women of all shapes, sizes and ages with little time and many other responsibilities? It seems impossible but there is, I discovered, an answer.

Until Nemesis, in the form of my first serious ski fall, caught up with me, I had culled a set of exercises from books, magazines and slightly embarrassed observations of racing teams in hotel corridors. No one seems happy being observed at their physical jerks. I am sure it is the same in most homes where one partner is on a set of waist-slimming exercises and the other is not. Once, while thumping out a ski race story for the *Guardian* in a Val d'Isère hotel, I was disturbed by a crashing and banging in the corridor which drowned my typing. Throwing open the door, I was startled to see a row of raised legs good enough for a Busby Berkeley film set. A dozen pairs of eyes stared up from the floor, faces pink from their exertions and growing pinker at the intrusion. 'Guten tag,

Österreich,' I uttered weakly, and hastily closed the door. Even the Austrian women's team, well used to physical training, hated an audience.

If group exercise – with its concentration and competition – is difficult for most, then the right place may be an unused bedroom. The right time is either first thing in the morning or last thing at night (when you can finish off with wash or shower). The right exercises I arrived at literally by accident. They have been evolved by Farnham Park Rehabilitation Centre, whose medical director, Dr John Williams, is secretary of the International Federation of Sports Medicine. For periods varying from three weeks to several months, Farnham Park rehabilitates industrial injury and motor accident cases of all descriptions, but its speciality is the injured athlete who requires a recovery process tuned to his condition. In general it needs to be as quick and intensive as possible, so that there is no deterioration in his general fitness while the ailing part – achilles tendon, cartilage, quadricep bone etc – is on the mend. The Centre reckons to release even Olympic class athletes considerably fitter than when they go in – Glynis Coles, after rehabilitation there from an ankle injury, played the best tennis of her life in helping Britain to win the Wightman Cup from the USA in 1975. Everyone – runner, tennis and soccer player, motor accident victim – graduates with a set of exercises which the Centre's enormous experience has taught will give the best possible benefit. These exercises will help every skier, and not only the first-timer.

Ski-ing is deeply demanding of mental and physical resources. People with serious worries rarely ski well. Tense, overtired muscles cause accidents. The Farnham Park exercises are convenient not only because they can be completed in fifteen minutes, but because they tone up the entire muscular system. There is also a distinct, measurable improvement in a matter of days. Skiers may be right in assuming that their leg muscles take the greatest strain. Farnham Park knows that even the little toe – important in ski-ing balance – is linked with muscular and nerve processes throughout the body. The fifth day after an achilles tendon operation they are giving you buttons to pick up with the toes, or a chalk stick which you grip between your big and your first toes to write your name on the floor. These exercises, with only the addition of ski (wall) sits, are the best I have met for strengthening and co-ordinating the muscle and balance sensors of ski-ing. They are best started a month before the holiday and then adhered to daily. During the grunts and groans it may help to bear in mind that Olympic athletes are set the same routines – and according to Farnham Park the average man or woman (one-third of their patients are women) quickly matches and sometimes excels a top athlete in his non-specialist fitness areas

		Repetitions
1	Press-ups, stomach not quite touching the floor in the down motion	15
2	Single sprint start jumps. Arms braced on the floor, legs straight out behind you. One leg then the other jumped up under the body, and back	20 each leg.
3	Step-ups onto a chair or stool, feet together, step down to the floor on the other side, then back to the original position	10 each leg.
4	Same as no. 2 but with both legs brought up under the chest into the squat position. Hips should be two inches from the floor when legs are straight	15

5 Lying on back, lift both legs about three
   feet from the floor, then lower   15
6 Star jumps. Starting in the squat position,
   leap off the floor throwing arms and legs
   out wide in a star shape, finishing in the
   squat position   15
7 Cycling. Shoulders on the floor, hands on
   hips, legs straight up in air, rotate legs as
   if cycling   50
8 Jacknife. Lying on the back, lift both legs to
   45 degrees, at the same time sitting up and
   touching your toes. Balance on the buttocks
   momentarily, then return to starting position.
   Ensure head and heels contact the floor at
   the same time   10
9 Ski sits. From standing position slide back
   down wall, and move feet away from wall
   until thighs are parallel to the floor. Hold
   there   60 secs
10 Burpees. Combination of no. 4 (double
   sprint start) and no. 6 (star jump)   15

Even the fittest may at first need some help with the
elbows after three or four efforts at no. 8, but this should
be unnecessary after about a week. It may take a week,
too, before fifteen burpees are possible. Some stiffness is
bound to be felt, especially in the stomach region. The
exercises may have to be trimmed at first, but you should
be doing them all before a ski trip.

Chapter 6
The Best-laid Plans...

All ice and snow sports carry a risk, if not for you then for someone else. If you hit another skier while overtaking, the skier suffers permanent injury and sues, and you are found responsible under the law of the land in which you were ski-ing; the third-party damages may run into many thousands of pounds. Only a madman, these days, skis without insurance, and all the leading British tour operators offer cover – some make it compulsory – at reasonable rates. The cover is similar for most: cancellation according to the price of your holiday, medical (which ought to be at least £1,250), loss or theft of personal effects and money (preferably £250 or more), and third party liability (not less than £25,000). Insurance can be taken through a tour operator, the Scottish National Ski Council or a firm like Douglas Cox, Tyrie (92 Fenchurch Street, London EC3; tel 488 3191) who provide a standard pack for Ski Club of Great Britain members or specialist service for those travelling independently.

I had skied off and on for twenty-two years before my first major accident. When it came the costs were as follows:

Blood wagon £16
Val d'Isère Clinic £16 (including four X-rays)
Physiotherapy £45
Nursing home £82 (four days at £16 per day
and £18 for the operating theatre costs)
Anaesthetist £31.50
Surgeon's Fee £183.75.

The National Health looked after costs for my three-week stay at Farnham Park Rehabilitation Centre, but mileage, some of which I could drive personally, some I could not, from my home in Sussex, was 1042. I had to take an early plane home via Gatwick, involving an extra cost of £42. The total, therefore, was well over £400.

The accident is worth retelling in some detail because falls happen to almost everyone, certainly to the beginner, to the skier trying to improve, to the tired person not aware how fatigue has crept up on him, to the distracted, and to the skier caught out by bad conditions or unsuitable equipment. Several positive lessons can be learnt from my misfortune: it was a combination of unsuitable equipment, distraction and tiredness, plus the bad luck of a style of fall which put maximum stress where I least wanted it. There was a build-up and a pattern, and with hindsight I could have broken the chain of circumstances at any one of several points. In other words, there was no-one to blame but myself.

I had sold a pair of long, 205-centimetre skis for the 1975–6 season and looked fairly deeply into the best type of short skis. Some friends had promised to bring up the skis I wanted from Austria, but for one reason or another they were unable to do so. Normally in Val d'Isère I am happy to hire, for early in the season the ST 650s and Rocs are in good condition, and I would have done so this time, but one of the friends concerned wanted me to try a pair of Atomic 175s – short long skis rather than shorties. The bindings were Salomon 555s, racer bindings with hard springs to prevent premature release at high speeds. I was clipped into these by a man who knows his bindings well, and we set them on the lightest setting. I did not at this point do two things that ought to be done: get someone to stand on the backs of the skis to see that I was released when I made a forward jerk with first one leg and then the other; nor did I hit the snow firmly with first one side of each tip, then the other, as a check for sideways release. I meant to do so, but what with the constant chit-chat of the first major ski races of the season, and the lack of a ski-ing companion in the short periods of free ski-ing before races, I did not get around to it. I would never make the same mistake again. The skis went pretty well, though lacking a little stability in the relatively short downhill running that I did even on the intermediate runs of La Daille. Turning was certainly easier, but there was a tendency to over-turn – that is, to make a sharper turn than my legs thought they were commissioning – but that was clearly a matter of practice and familiarity.

I did not have a fall for three days, and the fourth day, a Saturday, when I had no copy to file to my newspaper, broke beautiful and clear. It was a marvellous ski-ing day, the early-season snow still unspoiled, the pistes just used enough for whatever work-out was needed there. But the morning was full of premonition and tension. I had held onto a pair of four-year-old Garmont leather top boots with plastic soles because they were also comfortable for the job – standing about chatting at the bottom of racer runs, walking in the village streets to press centre and hotel. But the tread pattern had always been poor, just horizontal ridges and a density of plastic which sometimes had me slipping and sliding. They were far less stable than the crepe bottoms of my après-ski boots, or indeed than various other pattern-soled ski boots which I had tried at various times. I made a mental note to trade in the boots as I slid unhappily on the molehills and ridges of ice on the main road of Val d'Isère on this particular hard-frosted morning.

In a hotel I searched for a friend to keep me company. Ski-ing with someone else is not only a safety factor – a trip on a wood path with no-one around and one can lie unconscious, out of sight, with death from exposure more than a possibility – it also takes the pressure off your own performance. You are watching the other fellow or girl, prepared to lead if they are less experienced. Essentially, your mind is off yourself. The good days in ski-ing are when the body leads, the eyes searching out ground from fifteen to twenty yards ahead, picking a course and feeding it computer-like into the mind for the knees and lower legs to react. There is no introspection. There is no time or chance. You are ski-ing a bit faster than usual but firmly in control, not stopping to congratulate yourself or it might break the spell. Legs automatically ride small bumps and ridges because they are being reliably programmed. Everything is working.

Then there is the day when nothing is operating well; when the balance is poor, almost as if someone has filled the inner ear with treacle, when the visual signs are so slow or distorted that a modest fifteen degree slope becomes vertiginous or a huge, treacherous staircase, and the muscles shriek and protest at both the stairs that are not there and those that are.

This was such a day and I knew it going up in the téléphérique. It may come after a late or sleepless night, it may not. I only know that it comes, and I ought to be old enough now to recognise the symptoms and sit out in the sun with a good book and a glass of beer. Skiers,

however, are not made to give in, they just try to take
avoiding action. At the top of La Daille I decided to take
the longest, easiest motorway route in the whole Val
d'Isère complex – Grand Pré, which goes up and up to
a remote plateau, not dissimilar to Norwegian topography
if the jagged peaks round the rim are ignored. I looked
around for a liaison of convenience, and nodded to a
woman race official still coming up the tow.

To the left, people were taking off in the powder snow,
straight running about 100 yards to the piste. I followed,
thinking it might relax me. I tried a couple of weight
shifts but nothing much happened. Then I was onto the
pleasant, fairly gentle, if narrow, piste. 'Come on, nice,
easy, linked turns,' I told myself. Still I was jerky and
introspective. 'Bounce,' I ordered, wrongly. Bounce I did,
with my weight too far back on a swing to the right. My
right ski caught an edge and tipped me straight forward,
the ball of my foot grinding into the ski. Hell! The rear
binding was not opening. My left ski was now almost
alongside, and that did not release at the back either. I
felt a ferocious tug on both calves, then the left ski got
a sideswipe and opened, and I pivoted to a stop.

I knew it was bad. But how bad? I unclipped both
skis, and was relieved to find I could curl both toes. With
my sticks I tried to rise, but fell straight back into the
snow. The backs of my calves just felt gappy. Something
I had taken for granted was simply not working. The
woman official – a stranger, but she had a race armband,
as I did – skidded to a stop. She was about sixty, grey-
haired and concerned. The very presence I needed.

'C'est mal, monsieur?'

'C'est impossible d'aller, Madame.'

She took note of the posts at about 200-metre intervals
down the run. 'Numéro sept. J'appellerai les pisteurs
tout de suite. Bonne chance!'

I edge myself to the side of the run to avoid the possibility of a collision and more damage, and sit on my two skis to avoid as much cold as possible. In other circumstances I might have made a cross of them in the snow to alert other skiers. I check all my zips are done up to retain as much body heat as possible, keep my gloves on while doing everything up, and examine my predicament. Luckily I am still in the sun. Another 200 metres and I would have been in the shade – minus ten instead of minus two. I flex my toes and nothing feels broken. I shift my bottom slightly and the calves still feel oddly vacant. There is no panic. My mind gave an order and that part of me simply did not respond. Supposing no-one comes. I am in a vast room, blue ceiling, walls of white and beige, with here and there a fly or two. Not many. It is early season. No-one has passed by, come to think of it, and I have been here twenty minutes. Maybe the pisteurs are busy with the race practice. But surely the woman would have told them. They would have to come. Four figures fly by, heedless. Do they think I am sunbathing? Forty minutes now, and at last two stop – a man and a woman. Can they help? I tell them a woman has reported me, but some time ago. They say they will check and I am reassured.

Then I start to wonder how I could get down the half-mile to the start of the tow. Bumming it? No. Heels have no purchase. I think I might be able to swim, grabbing the snow in a kind of crawl, legs bent up double behind. There is always a rescue 'phone at the start of a tow. Down the far slope a fly takes an unusual shape. It is a man on skis towing a sled. He disappears behind a ridge and another quarter of an hour goes by. Was he for me after all? Just to my right he reappears, man and sled somehow towed by a soup plate. He waves, goes uphill of me for 200 metres, then detaches. It is a long slog over soft untracked snow before he is alongside. He is one of several dozen orange and black suited pisteurs on permanent duty over the 185 miles of pistes at Val d'Isère and Tignes.

I half explain the fall, half demonstrate with my hands. He pulls out a metal cage and fixes it to my right leg, accurately guessing damaged tendons, shortening and easing them by gentle screw pressure on the heel. He manoeuvres me into the canvas-slung sled and straps me in firmly; my feet are pointed up the slope, my head protected from his spray by a hood. He tows me the two miles to the bottom, puffing and grunting with his exertions. He tries to avoid the bumps but with one man it is awkward. My head strikes the metal hood frame painfully. Rather than yell I somehow free my arms and cushion my head with my gloved hands and fend off the hood frame with my elbows. A middle-aged man – do only the middle-aged have the time and understanding? – returns repeatedly to help him out. At last I am lifted into a waiting Safari ambulance. Within minutes I am staring at a clinic ceiling, white this time, and the steady, neutral eye of an X-ray camera. A doctor makes a preliminary examination and checks that I am insured. Then a male radiographer helps me off with my ski pants. A girl speaking careful English directs my legs for X-rays. I lie on my ironing board one hour, two. I am used to waiting now. Unbeknown to me, the great Swiss skier, Roland Collombin, is in another room with broken vertebrae.

The doctor re-emerges after examining all my plates and reports no breaks – only badly pulled muscles and tendons. He prescribes anti-pain and inflammation pills and bandages and leaves me to it. The clinic bill is 150 francs, or £16, which seems reasonable. My hotel is 100 metres away but it might be 100 miles. You cannot walk on a ripped tendon except like a man with tin legs, three inches forward at a time, every nerve screaming. The Swiss racing team doctor, born of English parents but never living in England, takes me there in his car. Colleagues do my packing, then lift, push and prop me against the wall as I am transported like a badly balanced doll to Geneva airport. British Caledonian are cajoled into putting me onto a charter flight to Gatwick at an hour's notice. Airport attendants wheel me to and from the plane, and my wife has been phoned and is waiting with the car at the airport. I could not wish for a more efficient and pleasant service.

The Val d'Isère clinic doctor's diagnosis of tendon damage was accurate, but his estimate of a fortnight off work highly optimistic. While there is so much swelling immediately after an accident it is hard to assess the true damage. The physiotherapist at home first gave me ultrasonic treatment, aimed at stimulating a restorative blood supply to the strained fibres of the calf muscle, and then Faradays, electrical impulses which tweak the calf. But the main trouble was in the Achilles tendon, just behind and above the ankle. This tough, elasticated fibre is hard to damage, but slow to heal if it is hurt. Many older skiers have suffered permanent impairment – usually a flat-footed walk – from damage to the tendon. Hard-shell boots coming higher up the leg have lessened the frequency of damage here, transferring stress to the knee – which can be worse – or fracturing the tibia just below the knee in particularly bad falls. Proper attention to bindings, ensuring that they open before damaging pressure builds up in a fall, avoids trouble in both areas.

The Achilles is slow to heal because it has the smallest blood flow in the body. Its bundles of fibre, known as collagen, use little oxygen, which is good when all is well, bad when it is not. It is appropriate that the expression, an Achilles heel, refers to a persistent weakness or frailty in an otherwise strong body. It is a problem for runners, who sometimes develop stress symptoms there, usually a granulation tissue or jelly which does not go of its own accord and slowly interferes more and more with the smooth leverage of the tendon, which is controlling the foot, ankle and leg functions. I was lucky that the outer tendon, which splices with the thicker inner tendon just above the heel, did not sever as it sometimes does, especially among the over-35s. When Colin Cowdrey, the England cricketer, went for a quick run one day and the tendon snapped, the report could be heard all over the field.

As the days went by it became clear that I could not rise on the balls of my feet because of the damage. Subsequently I twice missed my footing and sank back on my left heel in great pain. A further examination by one specialist at this point diagnosed severed tendons with the likelihood of three weeks total immobilisation in plaster on both legs, and walking on crutches for a further six weeks. But one of Britain's leading specialists in this field, Dr John Williams, operated on both legs and had me taking stairs two at a time within twelve days, something quite unheard of even five years ago. Providing the tendons are not badly or completely ruptured, he removes all internal scar tissue, clears out the granulation tissue which is not going to disperse naturally for perhaps six months to a year, re-sticks the membrane so the tendon is again moving smoothly under the skin, and steri-strips the operation scar so that the patient can begin work on the leg or legs within five days. It is a condition of his operation that patients attend Farnham Park Re-habilitation Centre, a National Health concern of which he is director, for up to four weeks remedial exercises – hard, almost unremitting work from 9 am to 12.30 and from 2 to 4 pm, in which Olympic athletes and road accident cases may be side by side, weightlifting, treading lathes, pulling physiotherapic springs or undertaking endless varieties of foot, ankle, leg and trunk movements.

Whatever fall, whatever accident a skier has after such an experience, it is unlikely to be without a much closer attention to the detail of his activity. If this is a reminder of ski-ing's perils, it can also relate to its bounty. Many of the remedial foot, ankle and leg exercises are prefaced with the words, 'Now imagine you are ski-ing', and we took a closer look at these in Chapter 5.

Chapter 7

On the Snow

Snow conditions vary according to the time of the season, day, location on the mountain, depth and age. Every few yards may have a different character to which the skier, first with his eyes if he is experienced, otherwise by the feel of the snow under his skis, must react. Great racing skiers must have this feel to an extraordinary extent. In one experiment, the Austrian Olympic downhill champion, Franz Klammer, was 'wired to the snow'. Over a set of runs his skis electronically recorded contact. It showed conclusively that his ski soles had a better contact than any other skier tested. The greater the contact, the larger the area and quantity of snow turning into globules of moisture, like millions of ball-bearings on which the ski rides. Thus the faster the skier will go. The beginner does not want to go as fast as Franz Klammer – eight miles an hour will do for him, not eighty. He has a fear factor which Klammer has long since forgotten. Tension and slowness create major problems for the learner – indeed, in varying degrees, for all standards up to the advanced. But every skier, eventually, must come to some sort of understanding and accommodation with the stuff he is ski-ing on.

SNOW TYPES AND DEPTHS

In choosing a particular time of year for a holiday, a skier has to reckon on the kind of snow condition he is likely to meet. In late December, January and early February there will be a predominance of cold, well-beaten snow, with Ratracs ploughing it up for easier ski-ing from time to time and snowfalls occasionally producing *powder* conditions which at first the beginner will hate. More than a foot of it requires a reasonable technique, strength, courage and confidence, and there is no way of acquiring this except through effort and guidance. Less than twelve inches may look formidable, but if a turn can sweep it away to the harder layer underneath, even the novice finds he can cope, and the intermediate discovers he is making the easiest and best turns of his life. Ski life is never so sweet as on those intoxicating mornings of sparkling new snow, a wide blue sky, a smiling sun and a phobia overcome. Later in the season, in late February, March or April, the novice will also meet *corn*, or spring snow, when the warmth of the sun causes a granulation just before and after midday. Before it becomes too mushy or freezes again, spring snow provides a superb surface for easy turning. There is not the hiss or spindrift of powder snow, but it is an even greater easer of tension.

Each day, each run, each section of run, as a skier soon finds, provides something different. As in a game of golf, you are never in the same position twice, no matter how familiar the course. You may think you know one of the longer runs – over a kilometre – backwards or blindfold. Along comes a better skier who takes you down faster than you have ever been, over a different line, and all is different. Even in good conditions, bottlenecks lower down will develop ice and rock. *Sheet ice* is the hardest of all ski surfaces. Soft snow may at least cushion a fall but glazed ice, with the rock blue-black underneath like a waiting shark, can make the toughest nerves quail. Usually you can get round it or find the patches of churned ice which will give you a better grip along your ski edges. At worst you take your skis off, but ski boot soles may be less well equipped for the job than skis. It is a consolation that almost everyone hates it, and if the experience teaches you to take your hire skis back to the ski shop for the edges to be sharpened, that may do wonders for your subsequent confidence and technique, always assuming there is no further heavy snowfall; a ski racer will in fact file his edges blunt for new snow. Sharp edges can dig in too far and cause a fall through catching an edge.

There are two other main types of snow to worry about – crust and porridge or mashed potato. *Crust* worries a beginner only in so far as he sees ridged or slabby snow, like a petrified sea, just off the marked run, and wonders what would happen if he ever lurched into that in a blizzard. The answer is that he would fall over, because the pressures under the sole of his skis (stiff, soft, stiff, stiff, soft, soft . . .) would totally nonplus him. A confident instructor with local knowledge could teach him how to cope with crust in his second or third year, but ski schools for the most part prefer to improve piste techniques. (Off-piste falls are usually time-consuming, with skiers having to struggle to get their skis back on in deeper snow, but a good school will still reckon to improve intermediates and advanced off-piste.) A crust is a layer of hard snow or ice on a softer base. Thin crust breaking under slight pressure causes little problem, but thick or variable crust, caused mostly by wind in exposed places, troubles even the experts. It is around all through the season. Beginners ought to know about it, but not give themselves nightmares. If they find themselves in it by accident they should pick the straightest path possible, even if it means swivelling on their bottoms to set their skis in the right direction.

Porridge, or *mashed potato*, or *crud* is what it sounds – snow in an advanced state of decay, so slushy it will wet you through if you fall in it. It is 'time to go home' snow, because there is no pleasure in trying to ski in it. Often it occurs through heavy rain, so there is little temptation to stay out in any case. Principally it is a danger at a low-lying resort at the end of the season – the eastern resorts of the USA suffer a lot in this respect, and so can the Scottish mountains.

Newspaper reports of snow depths on upper and lower slopes are important for those with the flexibility to vary their holiday dates and places at short notice, for those with a car and no firm booking, and for weekenders in Scotland. But for the best financial deal from an air package arrangement, beggars cannot always be choosers. January and early February are popular among Britons because they miss national and school holidays, prices are lower, the weather is often sunny in higher regions, although the snow is less ample than it was in the 'fifties, the low temperatures at this time of the year maintain what snow there is.

Human beings tend to see their own times in more vivid and extreme terms than longer-based studies, and this applies as much to snow climatology as any other. Unfortunately there is not much serious research on snow patterns over a meaningful period, which means that forecast and guidance must be qualified. It is possible to say that there was no November snow cover, even in the south of England, for forty or fifty years before 1962. Since then there has been at least one to two days. Britain's growing season is about nine days shorter in the middle 'seventies. There is evidence collected by the Climatology Department of the University of East Anglia of a cooling down of the land mass of ·2 to ·3 of a degree Centigrade over the whole year, and certainly of the winters, in Britain and Continental Europe. This does not seem much, but it has made quite a difference to the frequency, duration and spread of snow cover. Midwinters have been milder, with rather less precipitation, but there is a lengthening of the season in which snow is occurring. There is a different effect at different heights, with less obvious changes in the north of Britain than in the south. Elsewhere, moist winds off the Atlantic and Mediterranean have given the French Alpes Maritimes and Savoie, the French and Spanish Pyrenees and the Italian Alps more snow in some recent winters. Areas then suffering were the high central peaks of Switzerland and some of the Austrian resorts, though the Austrian weather pattern fluctuates enormously and Norway is less steady than it was. Scotland has had winters with little snow in January and February, but the cooler, longer springs have produced March and April blizzards, as in 1976, bad enough to cost the lives of walkers and to cause avalanches. Good snow prevailed all season in 1977. Heavy late snowfalls on a well-worn base have greatly troubled parts of the Alps, causing extensive damage at Saas Fee, Switzerland, in 1975. Late snow invaded a marked run at La Toussuire in the French Alps in 1976, and killed a former French international racer, Jean Pierre Augert. Lack of snow, rather than too much was the pattern, but in 1976–7 Europe had plenty while the Rockies starved.

The Ski Club of Great Britain has representatives at many resorts reporting daily for their service to newspapers. If they report less than six inches at resort level it means there is not much snow about. At higher levels less than twenty inches means the runs can be very dodgy, especially on south-facing slopes above the tree line, where the direct rays of the sun are bound to thin the snow and expose rocks. Early and late in the day it will be icy.

In general, the higher you go the better the ski-ing for intermediates and advanced. The slopes are probably – though not inevitably – steeper, but it will be colder. For beginners, who will often be watching and waiting or simply recovering breath, protected slopes at lower altitudes, possibly in wide, wooded glades where an element of shade will help retain good snow, are more appropriate. The Alpine tree line varies from about 5800 feet to 6500 feet, the higher figure applying on north faces out of the sun, but in truth mountains are irregular objects, with their faces, and therefore the longer ski runs, part in the sun and part out.

It is good to test out a travel operator's knowledge of a ski resort with questions on tree line, northern and southern faces, and the length and number of lifts. It wins attention and the extra nuggets of information which make all the difference in deciding between one resort and another. The assistants are only human. They have hotels to fill, but most are ski enthusiasts and will respond to intelligent and polite inquiry. Friends' recommendations are important, but take account of differing ski standards. The beginner learns more quickly with modern techniques and equipment, but a parallel skier, however sympathetic, will not be doing the same runs as a beginner. Be sure the friend is observant of the novice and his problems, in particular of the way a ski school operates, whether the classes are relatively small – a dozen is the rarely achieved ideal – and whether they seem to be enjoying themselves.

TURNING

A ski does its job more efficiently because of its shape. In plan view it is wide at the tail, narrower in the middle, and wide again at the shovel. It is also arched underneath the binding where the skier will bring most of his weight to bear. Standing normally the skier will force the arch, or camber, downwards. The effect is for the ski to track in a straight line. With more force still, the ski will bow in a reverse camber. The sidecut on the inside left ski will help a turn to the right, and vice versa. A skier gets the ski to turn in two main ways – by knee turning and by up and down motion. Mostly it is a combination of both. On flat snow, and given a certain momentum, he simply swivels his knees in the direction he wants to go and his flat skis, the sidecut or waisting ironed out by his weight, will turn in the appropriate direction. This, effectively, is the knee turn.

To explain in more detail how the skier uses the shape of his ski to turn, when he pushes his knees forward he puts more pressure on the front of his ski. The shovel will brake and with any sideways pressure the tail, which is not suffering the check, will fan out. This will start the ski turning in the direction to which its tip is pointing – in other words to the skier's left if the back of the right ski fans out right. The turn will be further reinforced when his weight comes back down under his foot – the higher the speed the quicker the weight transference back – because the sidecut section at the waist of the ski will now be bowing into the snow. The banana-shaped track being made by the inside edge is reinforcing the turning effect.

In softer snow conditions this effect will be more apparent than in hard; on ice there will be minimal bowing, or reverse camber as it is sometimes known, which is partly why ice causes such terror. Intermediate

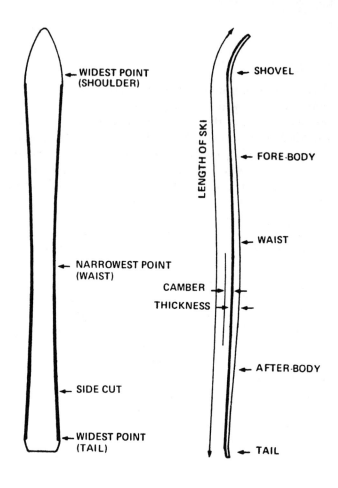

WIDEST POINT
(SHOULDER)

SHOVEL

LENGTH OF SKI

FORE-BODY

NARROWEST POINT
(WAIST)

WAIST

CAMBER

THICKNESS

SIDE CUT

AFTER-BODY

WIDEST POINT
(TAIL)

TAIL

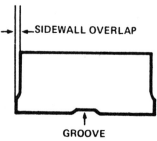

SIDEWALL OVERLAP

GROOVE

Fig. 6   Parts of the ski.

to expert skiers will also use the tails of their skis for a checking effect, bringing the ski tips round under control for a full turn, a slight directional change, a speed reduction or a stop. It is this particular use of the tails which brings about the parallel or hockey stop. When the learner skier achieves it he has broken an important psychological and technical barrier. It is essential to understand about modern ski-ing that, while the whole of the ski has a function, it is the critical three feet under the inside edge which controls turns. The beginner, in paralytic fright at the sensation of the sliding foot, tends to freeze into one position with only one part of the ski or edge employed.

Up and down unweighting needs explanation in detail, for it has a double, apparently contradictory, use and frequent misuse of the terms does not help. If you rise on your toes on a set of bathroom scales there is a brief moment when the downward thrust sends the weight needle up a few pounds. Then it flickers to something under your actual weight as you 'take off'. That, in ski-ing, is known as up unweighting. When you come back down again, helped by a small gravitational thrust, your weight briefly exceeds your actual poundage. That is downweighting. If you are standing on the scales and suddenly bend down, thighs parallel to the ground, the needle will flicker downwards. Very briefly you are less than your actual weight, and this is down unweighting. It is while you are unweighted, up or down, that you are reducing the frictional forces between ski and snow which are opposing your turn. This is the precise fraction of a second when you begin your turn. Then, as you come back down with distinct overweighting, the ski reverse-cambers, your weight thrust spreads along your inside ski edge, and you turn.

There are two main types of unweighted turn or, as it

is sometimes known, swing. They are the carve and the skid. If the edge bites sharply it is a carve. If it slips sideways with a fanning effect, it is a skid. If the waisting of the ski is considerable it will incline to bite and turn much quicker when the skier's weight comes down. This type of ski will be demanded by a racer of slaloms, the event many will have seen on television with its short, zig-zag turns between flagged 'gates' on a steep slope. The arch of a ski enables the skier's weight to be distributed along the whole length of the ski when he downweights. The spring back to the natural camber helps lift him in preparation for another turn. The more spring in the arch the better the ski will function. Top skiers will appear to rebound from one slalom gate to another, using their skis like sprung platforms. In effect, so they are. Less able but equally aggressive skiers may often be seen in a series of linked recoveries. The only advice is to get out of their way – fast.

The best way to start a turn is to point the skis directly downhill, towards the fall line in the ski-ing jargon, with gravity immediately reducing the friction which is stopping your skis from turning. Fear of the fall line is the first thing to overcome. You *can* turn on the flat, but only if you have built up sufficient speed from a preceding slope. Snow tends to get hard-packed or rutted where skiers hit the flat from a slope and it is easy to catch an outside edge in one of the shallow but deceptively hard ruts. Skiers soon learn to keep running straight in these sections and to pull up on an uphill section which they hope follows. If falling is the only answer, then it is better, within reason, to fall downhill. Even a few degrees of slope project you forward with far less of a thump than a tumble on the flat. If that thought helps to overcome slope shyness, so much the better.

There are sophisticated sub-divisions within a ski's

shape and design. A skier sufficiently experienced to go off-piste frequently, that is to tackle the soft snow, will certainly want skis with relatively soft tips so that they plane rather than dig into the snow. A longer ski is generally more suitable to soft snow, but surprisingly stable ski-ing is possible with Compacts, which preserve a high degree of flexibility in spite of their relative shortness.

The liveliness, or amount of flex, of a ski follows its method of construction, which I described in Chapter 5, rather than its shape. In 1967 I skied for the first time on a pair of skis with true spring – some brand new Head Masters, a derivative of the famous 'cheater' which had overcome its principal weakness, the rather floppy tips. Ski-ing suddenly felt a different game; they were tuned, responsive, and did what I wanted before I had formed a conscious thought. In other words I could go faster more safely, and the faster you turn under control the easier ski-ing becomes. The ascending spiral of confidence is checked only by sudden, difficult terrain or snowy conditions which demand a further set of values and responses. It is an important barrier to go through, though my pleasure was short-lived: the skis were stolen inside twenty-four hours.

The sequence of instructional drawings which follows has been specially drawn by Doug Godlington, Senior Trainer of BASI.

Basic sliding stance – skis apart for balance, legs flexed and hands held forward.

Stance for crossing the slope. The uphill leg and ski are pushed forward. Depending on the angle of slope the lower ski has more weight pressure. Outward lean of upper body from the hips.

Snow plough 'wedge' stance for elementary control at slow speed. Feet and skis are spread apart for balance with slight edging on inner side of foot. Knees are pressed towards tips. Wider 'wedge' angle gives a greater braking effect.

1. Basic stances

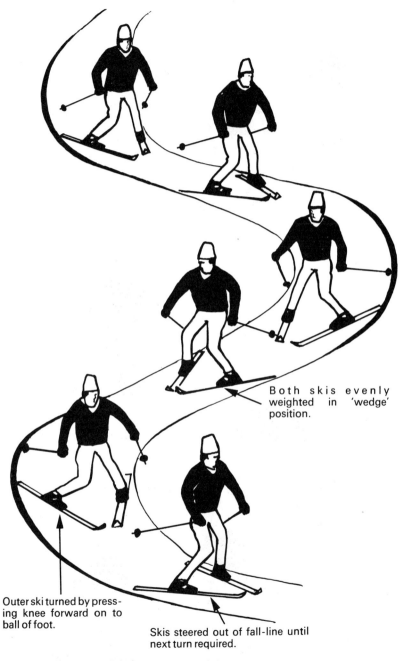

Both skis evenly weighted in 'wedge' position.

Outer ski turned by pressing knee forward on to ball of foot.

Skis steered out of fall-line until next turn required.

2. Snow plough turns

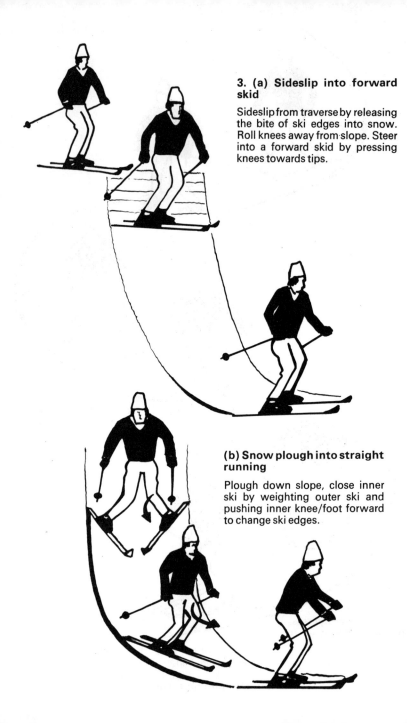

3. (a) Sideslip into forward skid

Sideslip from traverse by releasing the bite of ski edges into snow. Roll knees away from slope. Steer into a forward skid by pressing knees towards tips.

(b) Snow plough into straight running

Plough down slope, close inner ski by weighting outer ski and pushing inner knee/foot forward to change ski edges.

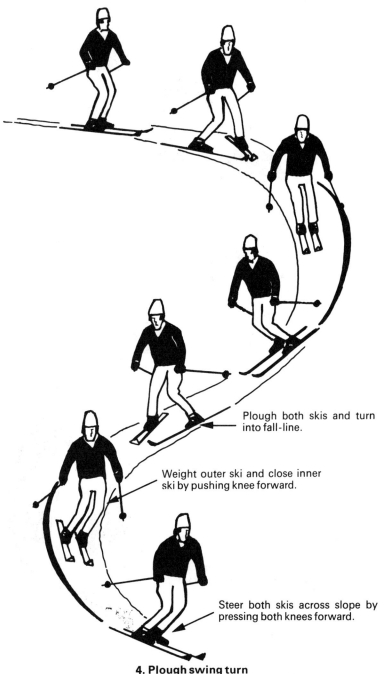

Plough both skis and turn
into fall-line.

Weight outer ski and close inner
ski by pushing knee forward.

Steer both skis across slope by
pressing both knees forward.

4. Plough swing turn

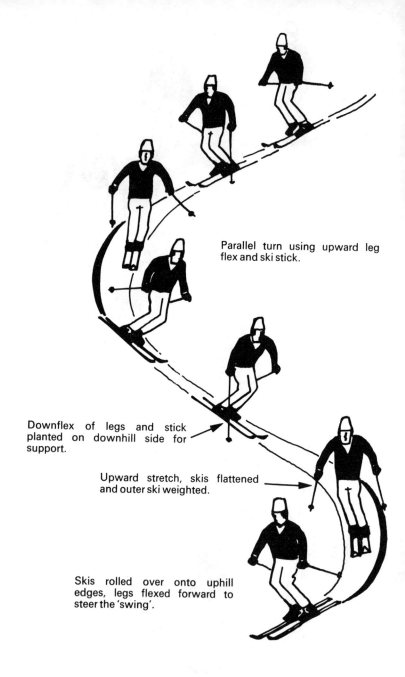

Parallel turn using upward leg flex and ski stick.

Downflex of legs and stick planted on downhill side for support.

Upward stretch, skis flattened and outer ski weighted.

Skis rolled over onto uphill edges, legs flexed forward to steer the 'swing'.

5. Parallel turn

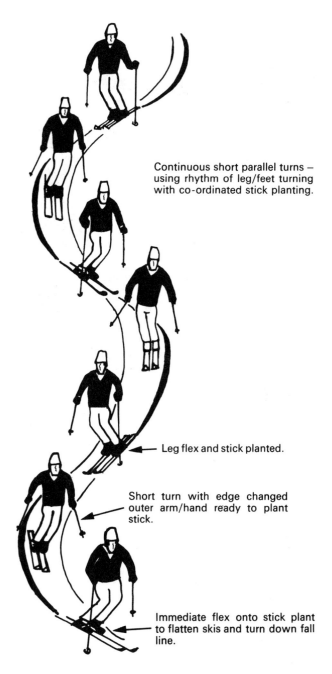

Continuous short parallel turns –
using rhythm of leg/feet turning
with co-ordinated stick planting.

← Leg flex and stick planted.

Short turn with edge changed
outer arm/hand ready to plant
stick.

Immediate flex onto stick plant
to flatten skis and turn down fall
line.

6. Linked parallel turns

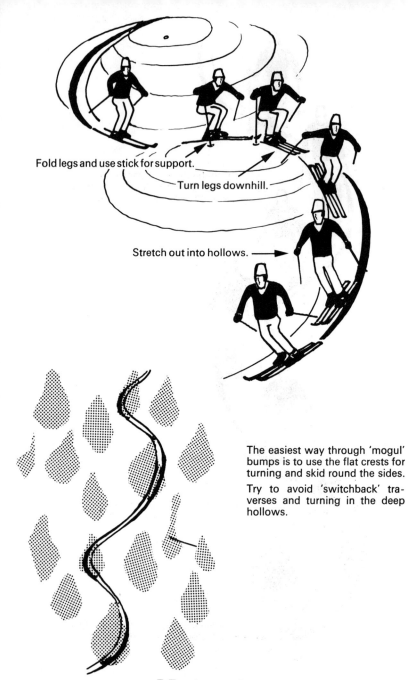

Fold legs and use stick for support.

Turn legs downhill.

Stretch out into hollows. ──▶

The easiest way through 'mogul' bumps is to use the flat crests for turning and skid round the sides.

Try to avoid 'switchback' traverses and turning in the deep hollows.

7. Turning over bumps

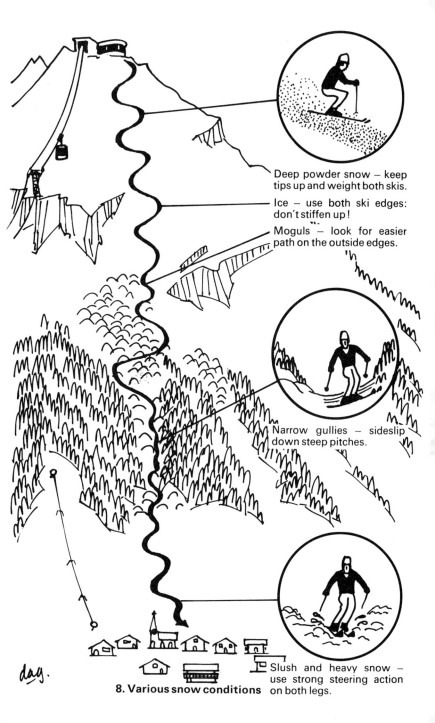

Deep powder snow – keep tips up and weight both skis.

Ice – use both ski edges: don't stiffen up!

Moguls – look for easier path on the outside edges.

Narrow gullies – sideslip down steep pitches.

Slush and heavy snow – use strong steering action on both legs.

8. Various snow conditions

dag.

SKI SCHOOL

Most schools divide their numbers into six classes. In Austria and France they start with Class Six and end up with Class One. In Switzerland the reverse applies.

The Beginners Class is for those who have never skied before, or who have just done a bit some years before. They will be taught how to put skis on, fix bindings and safety straps, hold their sticks, walk, climb by sidestep or herring-bone, how to get up from a fall, a kick turn, and a schuss.

Improving Beginners learn a snowplough position, turn and stop, linked snowplough turns or straight turns, traverse and sideslip. It sounds a lot, but most people learn them to various degrees in a week.

Intermediates are those who can snowplough reasonably and are getting the idea of a parallel stop. They do not automatically fall when a smooth, hard-packed run gets a little ridged, or possibly churned by a tractor. They are beginning to adjust to different depths of snow, and are learning to plot their tracks through terrain. It is here that skiers taught on plastic slopes have to learn new attitudes to a changing surface. They will be taken on runs of up to a kilometre.

Improving Intermediates will be instinctively adjusting to changing surfaces at higher speeds. They will have learned the various forms of stopping, including the swing turn into the hill, effective sideslipping and take-off into a turn, and will have gained more and more experience of snow, including powder. This is usually the biggest group at ski school because holiday skiers often reach this standard and stick for several seasons, if not forever.

Advanced skiers will be learning parallel turns and what it means to carve a turn as opposed to skid. They will be taken down steeper slopes, twenty degrees and more, and expected less and less to stem, which means fanning out their ski in a slight throwback to the plough turn.

Experts go from making parallel turns with a long radius to much shorter, linked turns in various snow conditions on the steepest of skiable slopes. They will need to learn snowcraft for occasions when they leave the piste and must judge avalanche slopes and other hazards.

Learning to ski is like learning to ride a bicycle. Once learned it is never completely forgotten, no matter what the interval of time, though the early sensations may give a momentary, light-headed 'What am I doing here?' sensation. Middle-aged men and women returning to the sport ought to be much encouraged. Most of the news is good. Equipment design is far better, the old hops and stems much easier to eliminate even for the over-forties.

For beginners, like Michael and Jenny, there is no basis of comparison. What is good instruction and bad? Good equipment and bad? What are the terms? Which are the most meaningful? Above all, will I keep my balance when I push off? The basic fear that has first to be conquered is that of the sliding foot, and anyone who has ice-skated, roller-skated, water-skied or, above all, skied on an artificial slope, is at once at an advantage. The fear has been put to the test and probably conquered. Half a dozen lessons on a plastic slope are worth the first week's holiday on snow. The sensation of sliding will have been recognised and mastered, the narrowness of the slope – rarely more than fifteen yards – will have encouraged a measure of control faced by the fall line, which for many beginners is exactly that, though it should not be. The fall line, being the steepest and most direct line down a slope, has to be exploited in any turn.

In his early days, whether on plastic or snow, the beginner will have a run-out section which his instructor will ensure gives him ample time and room to slow down and stop without the use of turning technique. After a time a skier will be able to size up for himself how much stopping or turning area he has. It is a weakness of many ski schools that they do not allow enough early opportunities of straight running. Half a dozen runs of 50 to 100 metres down a gentle nursery slope ought to precede any attempts to turn. They release tension, encourage instinctive individual reaction from the legs, and, quite incidentally, teach an element of steering. It is at a later stage of the learning game, on more testing slopes or more difficult snow conditions, that you learn the wisdom of the reconnaissance. No experienced skier of any wisdom 'bombs' a strange run. First he reconnoitres it and slowly, as he grows more accustomed to it, lets his skis go. If that is the case with the world's top racers – and they all spend four full days reconnoitring a downhill, even if they have raced it many times before – it should also be the case with skiers right down to the learner.

METHODS OF TEACHING

The US Graduated Length Method and its French equivalent, Ski Evolutif, and Orthodox learning such as the New Austrian System, are often presented as rivals, with the first two concentrating on short skis. Closer examination shows them as fruits at different points of growth and exposure on the same tree. It is no coincidence that the Graduated Length Method, which starts the novice on skis one metre long, with the bindings set well back and the arching less pronounced, has developed on the flat, groomed slopes of the USA and the purpose-built French resorts. The Americans, especially, deploy extensive snowmaking, daily grooming, bulldozed, purpose-built runs, highly articulate instruction, and efficient, detailed organisation. What it comes down to is a snow carpet for beginners which gives them immediate confidence to knee-swivel their skis in a parallel or wedge shape. The novice instinctively realises that a shorter ski means less leverage if he falls, the fear factor is quickly conquered, technique advances rapidly and, under controlled conditions, the skier is introduced to more demanding snow and slope variations with a longer ski appropriate to the job.

The longer skis will have a pronounced arch for the more sophisticated turns which at that point will be necessary. Conventional European instruction, such as the Austrian National system, starts skiers on the longer ski and from the word go encourages an up and down motion in concert with the knee swivelling. The arch and sidecut of the ski are at once employed in the build-up to 'unweighted' turns. The skier will be taught to get the feel of his inside ski edges on both legs, and the use of each leg independently. By 'longer ski' I mean 160 centimetres and above for women, and 170 and above for men, although this is somewhat arbitrary. It embraces most Compacts. Continental ski schools usually accept skiers with even shorter skis, but it ought to be explained that the teaching method is not geared to them. The longer ski is undoubtedly better adapted to their requirements.

Most countries claim their individual styles, especially those with major tourist industries, which in the Alps means Austria, Switzerland, France and Italy. However certain evolvements applied to. all. In the 1960s and 1970s the word 'swing' was increasingly used as an English expression to signify change of direction rather than the word 'turn'. Strictly they are not interchange-able, but the onomatopoeic implication of swing, a more gradual, arcing turn, better suited the designs of the ski instructor in the earlier stages of instruction. The plough turn was relegated in importance and, by the middle 1970s, increasing importance was placed on the use of legs independently and adaptation to changing terrain.

Austrian basic teaching falls into four parts: walking; running in the fall line; snowplough and snowplough turn (sometimes spelt snowplow); and basic swing. The instructor brings in traverse, sideslip and uphill swing as he thinks appropriate to his pupil's progress.

Karl Gamma, of Switzerland, in promoting various Inter-Ski Congresses, has tried to encourage a unified European teaching method without success. The Austrian, French and Swiss methods arrive at the same point eventually, but usually with different emphases at different points. Each country's tourist industry demands selling factors, and a teaching system becomes part of it. The French thought they had stolen a march with the success of their racers led by Jean-Claude Killy and Marielle Goitschel, using avalement, or jet, techniques which make much more use of ski tails. But in part this was due to improved ski design, as I have explained, and in any case was mostly for racers and advanced skiers. The French, led by Joubert, certainly encouraged less upper body movement than the Austrian style of the late 'fifties and 'sixties, which over-emphasised counter-rotation, or the amount the upper body has to compensate for leg movement by turning against it.

In the French turn the outside arm and shoulder are carried through to lead the rest of the body, and the body is pointed in the direction of the turn all the time. As he goes through a turn, the French skier throws his outside arm forward in an automatic banking motion. (So, incidentally, does the Swede, Ingemar Stenmark.) The French stand more erect. Everywhere else in the Alps the turn is taught with the chest pointing down the slope. You stand with your feet together, then turn your body until your shoulders face to one side and lean over in that direction. Your weight automatically rides on to the outside foot.

The Austrian technique is less accentuated now, and in places merges with the French. Chest pointed down the slope is certainly right for turns, but not, inevitably, for traverse across slopes. A kink in the side is often enough to put weight on the downhill ski, with your chest facing the way you are going. The other major adaptation common to both schools concerns technique over moguls – the bumps caused by repeated passage of skiers over the same spot, usually the steeper section of a run. At one time skiers were simply encouraged to turn on the banks of the bumps as best they could, which was all very well until they became icy and rutted and over-used. Most schools now encourage turning on the tops of the bumps (it helps keep the bumps down, incidentally) with a sinking motion on top of the bump, a swivel, then a stretch as you slip into the trough.

The Austrian system goes on to more advanced forms; turns with skis parallel (parallel swings), short, linked turns (wedeln), and one-legged push-offs into turns (step-over swings), the last reflecting the sort of slalom turn introduced by the Italian champion, Gustav Thoeni. Basic instruction tries to induce these in rough form, with the skier improving his confidence and style by repetition, minor experiment and a rising bank of knowledge which fits the right instinctive response to a new situation.

Just how far ski technique and instruction should be a conscious affair is a big topical debating point. In America 'Inner Ski' is the rage. The game is to make a skier's body sense take over, to turn off the verbal mind. The instructor does not tell a class where the weight should be on the ski. He asks 'Where is your weight? You tell me.' Skiers learn better by example, it is claimed, not by being told wrong from right. The debate is never-ending, but most adults crave logical explanation as part of their learning pattern, and the more intelligent they are the more they are inclined to seek it. The dynamics of a ski ought to matter for any understanding of the sliding foot although, as with gear-changing a car, the sooner it passes into the unconscious mind the better. To quote Frederick Deane, GLM supervisor at one of America's biggest ski centres at Stratton, Vermont: 'In normal situations, in a given time span, an adult who can accept verbal instruction will learn to ski much faster than a child who can only attempt to imitate.' On the other hand, most children will not stand for lengthy explanation, and a good demonstration at a given moment can have a remarkable effect. To illustrate that point, Norm Crerar, Director of Ski-ing at Mt Snow, Vermont, on a 'Watch me' principle took his novice class straight into a series of linked turns while explaining only in Swedish, which none of the class understood. He found that the weaker ones improved their turns immediately.

I must report that in a basically self-taught ski life I have much valued specific tips, explanations and demonstrations. The timing of the advice, whether visual or verbal, is what is important. We cannot see ourselves – those resorts with video-tape instructional services are on to something – and bad habits creep in just as they do at golf or any other game. If someone can show me what I am doing wrong, and then the exercise to get me out of the habit, I am only too pleased. That kind of hand-tailored instruction, at one time hard to acquire from an English source, is increasingly available thanks to the encouragement of British based instruction on the artificial slopes and in Scotland. All countries have evolved learning systems to suit their physical conditions and economic circumstances. GLM and Ski Evolutif, with the need to change skis at precise stages, can work only where the ski school is linked with the ski hire shop. This rarely happens in Austria, Italy, Switzerland and the first and second generation French resorts. Ski Evolutif is superior in principle to the older forms of instruction, which are not so consumer orientated, but it is basically learning-made-easy for the fortnight-a-year holidaymaker. It is not the way an Arlberger or, come to that, a Carrbridge, Scotland, youngster learns. He absorbs snow feel and craft over a much longer period, and gets the repetitive experience which is part of all learning processes. To become expert, those taught GLM must still make the switch, within or outside the system, to up-and-down weighting which gives them mastery of their inside edges.

CROSS-COUNTRY SKI-ING

No picture of present-day ski-ing can be complete without reference in detail to Nordic ski-ing. It is the parent-turned-orphan now rightfully restored to the top table. Traditional Norwegian ski-ing is now back in favour in the Alps, North America and Scotland, partly for itself, partly for its cheapness. Uphill transport for downhill ski-ing is as big a component in a ski package holiday as the air fare from London or Manchester to Zurich. Dispense with the need to ride up hills by climbing them yourself, and the saving is self-evident, especially for families.

Olympic Games television pictures of lusty athletes striding out kilometre after kilometre give an inaccurate picture of the activity as it is practised in Scandinavia or

Continental Europe. Racers use a much heightened technique compared with the Norwegian families out for a stroll in their own woods and hills. Alpine and North American cross-country ski-ing has also been adulterated to some extent by the brash marketing techniques employed for downhill ski-ing. 'Langlaufers live longer' or 'Get fit on a Loipe' is a Madison Avenue approach to an activity which has no need of it.

These days it is possible to spend large sums on super-lightweight plastic touring skis with fishscale soles ('Give your wax back to the bees'), fashion knickerbockers, calf shoes and so on, but you will look a little silly in Hovda, Geilo, Nordmarka or Lilliehammer in such a fashion-conscious get-up. Norwegians tend to wear all-purpose cagouls in muted colours, and knickerbockers and stockings that they will also wear while out shopping. In the Alps, langlauf, ski-wandering, ski touring, Nordic ski-ing, langrenn, mean much the same – you ski well-marked courses, usually called loipes, of specific length and height variation. In Scandinavia you set out on mountain or forest walks – probably a bit of both – where the intention is to discover the wilderness, to let its silence enter the soul, or its wild life gently brush the spirit. An Alpine ski-ing drop-out, someone who has never reached the top of any given tow, can still enjoy this basic experience on Nordic skis.

The equipment is simple. Ordinary flared ski pants and an anorak are not scorned. Lightweight shoes, skis and sticks may be hired for about £10 a week even at 1977 rates of exchange. Ratrap bindings have three studs and shoes have three corresponding holes in the front of the soles. The foot is slid into the binding, you position the studs into the holes, and clip the binding spring onto the front welts. The toe is thus secured while leaving the heel free to be lifted and lowered. Sticks are gripped exactly as in Alpine ski-ing, though they tend to be longer. Waxing of skis is a bit of a problem. The hire shop will have them prepared for conditions when you hire. The next day may see temperatures rise or fall, calling for something else. But getting to know the various colours of waxes for differing temperatures, learning how to spread it over the ski soles, how to scrape it off for a reapplication or a bit of a mix; this is part of the fun. For recreational purposes, Swix make only two waxes, one for cold conditions, the other when the snow becomes warmer and more granular, and this simplifies matters.

The more skilled touring skier has a relaxed, easy stride with rapid pushing movements plus long glides with the weight first on one ski then the next. Eyes focus about fifteen metres ahead, and not on the ski tips. One arm plants the pole while the opposite leg pushes down and back in a horse-kick motion, providing the 'push' for the other leg to glide forward. The pole is a balance factor. The forward force is in the kick. Once gliding stops a touring ski, properly waxed, will stick until the weight comes over the top and the kick is applied once again to create forward pressure. Arms should swing close to the body, hand almost brushing the knee as it swings the pole forward. Double-pole pushes help increase speed on slight downhill stretches. Turns are executed much as in ice skating, pushing off from an angled ski which is then swiftly brought parallel. Uphill the stride is much shorter. Backward slide can best be arrested by picking up the ski and planting it firmly down. It is worth carrying the two types of waxes, for snow conditions will change as one climbs. Downhill it is usually possible to glide in tracks without fear of speeds becoming dangerous or of the track not levelling out. Skating turns, or the stem christie, can be made downhill. Edge control is not nearly as precise as with Alpine skis, and it is important not to try and stem when in tracks – which is advice for all types of ski-ing, for it is all too easy to catch an outside edge and go tumbling forwards. Soft snow in gentle Norwegian terrain is highly inviting, the most sensuous of all ski-ing experiences. Even a beginner will be able to enjoy it.

JENNY IN THE SNOW

Jenny's first gulp of Alpine night air as they step off the coach is sharp and scourging. It is a subtly exciting sensation: the first sign of challenge from a totally new environment. As she unpacks in the mellow warmth of her room, she is grateful for the advice of Brian and Ann. They have packed to a fourteen-day plan, assuming twelve days on the snow.

SKI WEAR

	Trousers	*Anorak*	*Gloves/ Mitts*	*Hat*
Jenny	One (salopettes)	One	One pair	Two (woolly and fur)
Michael	One	One	One pair	One (woolly)

UNDERWEAR

	Vest	*Pants*	*Tights*	*Bra*	*Socks*
Jenny	None	Four	Three	Two	Two pairs thick
Michael	Two	Three (one long)			Two pairs thick, three thin

TOPS

	Polo necks	*Sweaters*	*Shirt/Blouse*
Jenny	Four (two dressy)	Two thin, one thick	Two
Michael	Two	Two thin, one thick	Two (open-neck)

APRÈS-SKI – OUTDOOR

	Snow Boots	Top coat
Jenny	One pair (fur/thick fleecy lining)	One (fur/nylon fur/ heavy wool)
Michael	One pair	One (suede, lined jacket)

APRÈS-SKI – INDOOR

	Skirts	House shoes	Dress	Jacket	Trousers
Jenny	One long, one denim (short)	One pair	One (short)	One	One pair slacks, one pair jeans
Michael		One pair		One	One pair slacks, one pair jeans

Both have brought soap, which is not always provided in Austria, and Michael has a Continental adapter for his electric razor, which operates between 120 and 220 volts.

Jenny has brought a lighweight blow-dryer and styling brush, knowing she has to take her hairdo under a shower and into a swimming pool – even middle-grade Austrian hotels may have their hallenbad so both Michael and Jenny have brought their swimming things. She also has an easy hairstyle for pulling a woollen hat on and off, and will not suffer the flyaway problems of altitude where the hair literally follows the brush. She has a good shampoo and conditioner, and face and hand creams and moisturisers to cope with sun and wind tans. Nails are going to take a hammering, hand and toe, so all are trimmed shorter than usual, and scissors are a must. Ann recommends nail cream which will help nails subjected to much fumbling with clips and clasps, and made more brittle by altitude. Sun creams are now on the market which are far less greasy than those at one time thought necessary for mountain protection, also lip salve which ought to be applied under lipstick then reapplied during the day. Essential medicaments include aspirin or paracetamol (glare produces the occasional headache), a small quantity of milk of magnesia or indigestion tablets, and band-aid in case of raw ankles, toes or broken nails. Skiers liable to herpes should also take a small tube of Blisteze or an equivalent. £100 spent on a trendy ski outfit is money down the drain if the disfigurements of altitude hit those who are vulnerable.

Jenny finds kitting out before ski school reporting time – 9.30 or 10, though first-timers are advised to check in earlier – both an excitement and an ordeal. Sometimes it is done in too much haste, with the novice meekly submitting to an assistant who speaks little English and concerned only with keeping things moving. All the same there are musts.

Skis

Brow to head high for a Compact, above head high for a Standard, twenty centimetres below body height for Shorts. Compacts are usually 69–71 mm wide, Standards 66–69 and Shorts 74. They must have reasonable edges. Feel the new skis on display. They should be sharp enough to pare a nail – in theory, anyway. Compare them with what you are offered and if necessary ask for a sharpening (which does not take long). The arch or camber is best tested by placing the skis sole to sole, tails on the ground, and squeezing them together with the thumb and two fingers. There should be no gaps between shovel and tail, and when released the skis should spring back into position. If they feel sloppy and fatigued, ask for another pair. Examine the soles for gouges which, under the binding especially, can affect tracking. It is the edges under the binding which carry much of the weight. See that these are not burred.

Poles
These are much taken for granted but the precision with which they are planted will matter a great deal to a beginner learning to climb or to get himself up after a fall. Later on, they will assist in the timing of turns. I prefer a shortish stick, the top ten to twelve inches below the armpit with the point on a hard floor. On the snow, of course, the point digs in up to the basket, two to three inches above the point. The basket designs vary: the sort with circular looped patterns can catch in boot clips, and I prefer a heavy-duty plastic design. Ski poles are made with a high centre of gravity, and should feel almost wand-like. Badly worn straps should be avoided. You push your hand upwards through the loop and grasp the head of the pole, enclosing the inside of the straps. The poles will be controlled by the four fingers, with the thumb in a sling made by the inside strap.

Bindings
These are the make or break element of ski-ing – at times quite literally. There can never be enough care and watchfulness over them. Experienced skiers service them with white spirit cleanser, use a pipe cleaner to get round pivot points and into cracks, and spray them with protective silicone. They will also be totally familiar with their settings. Good ski shops at home will offer machine testing (another case for buying or renting in Britain), but I have never been offered this in a Continental hire shop. In general, the French are the most careful, and

are rarely content to check binding pressures simply with a knowing cuff of the hand. In many French resorts, you will mount a platform with a pair of parallel bars and, after the heel bindings have been set, will be told to jerk forward. The heel of the boot should release from the back binding. No matter how the rental shop impresses you, a similar test ought to be made with a friend standing on the back of first one ski and then another. If you push forward hard with the knee you should release. Another test for the front binding is to cuff the snow with first one then the other side of the shovel of both skis. If they come out very easily, take them back for moderate tightening, remembering that for a beginner it is better to release too readily than not at all. If they do not release, they need a lighter setting. Usually settings are from one to five, one being the lightest. Some have a colour code which needs checking with the maker's instructions or the rental shop. Some modern bindings have built-in ski stoppers, but hire shops are usually a year or two behind the most modern equipment (some, regrettably, are more like five years). Again, the French set the best standards among Continental countries, although Austria has made big efforts to modernise itself. Most skis will have retaining straps fitted to the rear binding which clip or hook round the ankle. They must never be left loose or they may work under the ski sole.

Leaving the rental shop, Jenny remembers Brian's advice to tie her skis together, sole to sole, with the straps in a loosish knot. Ski toting is annoyingly difficult for a beginner. Ski shops usually provide a rubber clip to keep them together, but all too soon this seems to get lost, gloved or mittened hands fumble around and the skis start to scissor. For a short walk, holding the skis vertically with your hand just above the binding and using them like a giant walking stick is one way of going on. The other hand uses both ski poles as the other stick. Otherwise it is best for a right-handed person to balance skis on the left shoulder, tips forward, binding just behind the shoulder, hand paw-like as far down the blade as is comfortable. Some prefer the skis laid on their edges to avoid knobbly bindings digging into the shoulder or ripping the stitching of their anorak. Good padding on the shoulder matters here. Setting the skis down requires care, or an innocent bystander gets a nasty clout.

All organised ski schools have a reporting point on the nursery slope with notices where newcomers or different classes of skier should foregather. It is important to allow time to get tickets from the ski school office if you are not provided with them under a package arrangement. Children from about twelve upwards are normally included in adult beginner classes. Jenny and Michael are in a mixed bag of a dozen beginners, middle-aged, young and adolescent, some quiet and self-absorbed, others looking for a smile or acknowledgement of a shared experience. Most are German-speaking, but with a far better knowledge of English than an equivalent English group would have of German. Jenny's instructor's English is adequate, and he quickly establishes who speaks what.

Putting on the skis is the first test. Jenny remembers to scrape and bang the snow off the first boot with her ski stick. Brian has told her how crusted snow under the boot can prevent the welts sliding under the front and rear binding lips. Even a small amount may interfere with the 'feel' of boot sole on the ski and make balance that much more difficult. At worst, it will tip her out of her binding prematurely. She is not at such altitude that her heart pumps just at the effort of bending down, but she finds she has not opened the rear binding (it is the type that swivels up like a miniature Tower Bridge) and has to get her ski stick point to poke the rear flange down and release the spring.

She holds herself steady with her poles and pokes her toe under the front binding flange, positions her heel over the sprung jaw of the rear binding, then drops her weight on it. There is a satisfactory clunk, and she looks down to find her boot positioned straight on the ski (it is important not to have the toecap slightly askew). She does up her safety strap clip, then tries to repeat the process with her left foot. But by now she is suffering her first experience of sliding foot. Her right ski skids forward even as she tries to position herself. The ground she is on is not as flat as she thought, and only a stab with a ski stick stops her from falling. She finds herself beginning to tremble slightly with the effort of balance and bending. The snow is hard and slippery in this well-worn part, but a couple of yards to the side it is softer. She makes a platform in it with the ski she wants to put on, finds she has more stability there for the ski she is already wearing and positions her boot over the binding again, making sure that the rear jaw is open. She puts her toe in the front binding, pressing lightly downwards rather than forwards, and pushes down hard with her heel. She clicks in, checks the boot and ski alignment, does up the safety strap and looks round, flushed but a bit happier. She suddenly remembers that she has her ski boots semi-clipped for walking down the street, and tightens them.

Michael is struggling into his skis still, so Jenny starts a few sliding steps towards the sign where the beginners are gathering. Her feet feel heavy and the bindings which stop her lifting her heel are like a rat-trap. Ankles accustomed to some sideways movement have little or none when the knee is pushed forward. Now they act only as hinges between legs and skis. Michael is learning a different lesson. It is necessary to position the ski across any slope so that it will not run away. Some like to use both hands when putting on skis, others like to position themselves using poles. It depends on snow and slope and becomes a matter of experience.

Good schools begin with warm-up exercises, jumping up and down or hopping, one leg then another, not only to get the circulation going but to stop the 'wooden leg' sensation developing. Man is a biped, each leg working independently of the other with muscular shock absorbers in his calves, thighs, buttocks and back helping him to keep balance. If these stiffen they cannot do their job. The sooner each leg is felt to have a different operation the quicker a skier develops confidence.

The first short run-downs are achieved not by going up a lift but by climbing. Jenny finds her skis slipping back as she tries to walk up even shallow gradients. She can get round this by diagonally sidestepping, digging in the uphill ski edges a bit so that she does not run back, or, when the gradient is too much for that, either side-stepping up in a straight line or herring-boning. This is what it sounds like, skis in a V, tails not quite touching behind her, knees tucked in a bit to ensure the inside edges bite, then going up a slope, one ski after the other, splay-footed. The ski pole is planted behind as she pushes off with first one ski and then the other. Even in sophisticated turns, ski poles are for pushing off rather than leaning on. It is a fine distinction, but it can make a lot of difference to performance. Two points Jenny has to remember. Her hand over the top of the ski pole, butt cradled in the palm, helps with the push-off. Both in herring-boning and in sidestepping upwards, she thinks of knee, ankle, foot and ski as one solid block lifted by the thigh. She finds the best sequence, according to the degree of slope, is walking, sidestepping diagonally, herring-boning and sidestepping directly upwards, the bottom ski being drawn up underneath the top one in a series of steps, the poles in constant use for checking and leverage.

Starting to go downhill has its problems. Jenny finds herself starting to slide with her body all wrong and her skis not quite parallel, and promptly sits down. She does so in the best possible way, sideways and back, hands out of the way. She can only sit and laugh, which is no bad way to relax before getting up. Too many skiers, like boxers, are on their feet before they are ready, perhaps before they have checked that their bindings are not undone. Jenny, still on her bottom, swings her skis down the slope and positions them at ninety degrees, edges dug in a bit, before pushing herself up with the help of her poles. Skis rarely come off at this sort of speed, but when they do the drill is to stick the tail of one ski into the snow and step into the other. Always wedge the ski into the snow on the downhill side, having released the retaining strap, but even on a ledge or depression treat it like a live thing, ever ready to slip away.

Skiers must get themselves organised in personal details and in the mind. A composed start is essential to ski-ing at any level and sets the tone for the entire run whether it is fifty yards or two miles. Beginners so often start off before they are ready. The confidence which a short straight run can give is enormous. You do not necessarily shoot downhill like a bullet, though eight mph may at first seem like that, and an uphill pull-up the other side shows how terrain can be used to check speed without turning or checking techniques. Jenny prepares for her first straight run – universally known as a schuss – by sidestepping up, then, skis edged across the slope, turning chest down to the way she wants to go and sticking in both poles about two feet apart. Leaning on her two poles, the butts now pressing into her palms, so that arms and sticks form a rigid line, she carefully moves her skis round so that they are facing downhill. The dug-in poles continue to hold her safely, and she thinks about the position she wants to be in, the basic downhill posture, before she lets herself go.

Skis should not be tight together but shoulder wide or a little less. Jenny remembers to look ahead and not at her ski tips. Her hands hold the ski poles in a comfortable but fairly low position, much as she might hold an extra-wide driving wheel. Even in turns, later on, she will be reminded of this analogy. The whole of the foot should feel the bottom of the boot, not just the balls of the feet. Hip, knee and ankle should be slightly flexed. Over a bump, or on a patch of sticky snow, a little more bending of the knees is all that is necessary, and all the other balance muscles in thigh, buttock and lower back will come into play. In a dip or hollow just stretch the legs into it, but still keep the knees relaxed. Stiff legs make the bottom stick out and the upper body lean too far forward.

It is really very hard to fall over the ski tips. Sitting too far back makes you go faster but out of control unless you are highly experienced. If in trouble, Jenny pushes her knees farther forward – the answer to a great variety of ski-ing situations. Quickly her instructor introduces bend and stretch movements in straight running – touching the sides of the boots, bending under a horizontal ski stick, making the knees rock. She learns skating steps, pushing off right then left, then touching first the right boot top then the left as she runs downhill. All are exercises teaching flexibility, the use of the legs independently, and what happens with up and down movement.

By day two her instructor is introducing the kick turn. Michael finds to his chagrin that it is all but impossible with his long body and short legs; his proportions are all wrong. Jenny, with her long legs, finds it quite easy. The kick turn is the most basic safety device in ski-ing. It is used where the skier goes off the main track and comes to a stop in deep snow, or is on a particularly severe slope where he does not dare perform a conventional moving turn. Jenny is taught it first on the flat. Starting with the skis side by side, left pole forward, right pole back by the tails, she lifts her right ski vertically with its tail touching the ground or even half an inch in the snow. Using the tail as a pivot, she twists her right ski so the skis are parallel or nearly parallel again, but pointing in the opposite directions. Leaning on the right pole, Jenny then swings her left ski through 180 degrees to bring it parallel again with her right ski. It is quite a contortion, and the elderly, those with difficult body proportions, or simply those with suspect knee cartilages, are not advised to try beyond a reasonable point of stretch and strain. Those who can do it, even with a bit of effort, undoubtedly have an extra safety factor in their ski-ing lives. Once accomplished on the flat it can be practised on a slope, using the uphill ski to turn on, chest down the slope in the course of the turn and both poles backwards into the hill. The main rule is to keep the knee doing the turn as relaxed as possible.

Quickly exploiting the first glow of confidence, the instructor takes his class to a lift. These are of two main types on a nursery slope – the T-bar and soup plate or button, pulled by lines attached to an overhead cable. Many places now have automatic lifts, but for a first ride the instructor should supervise. The button is attached to the line with a bar. Jenny positions her skis with the tails against a back board, skis about eight inches apart, holds her two poles in one hand and takes the bar with the other. The movement of the bar towards her (some come from behind) triggers the mechanism which, after a pause for her to slide the plate between her legs and make herself comfortable, pulls her up. The initial jerk is bigger on long tows than on the short ones on the nursery slopes. The temptation to sit down on the button has to be resisted. Jenny is told to relax the knees, keep the feet a little forward, hold on to the bar with one hand, and let it pull her. T-bars double the uphill capacity, carrying two at a time, but pose more problems for beginners since one skier can upset the other. An arm round the other's waist is not only cosy, it is the right way to distribute weight. Shoulder to shoulder is right. The one great mistake is to lean outwards.

Skiers learn a great deal from tow tracks. The more they relax the easier it is, even when it comes to corners on much longer tows where formidable pits develop in spite of the attendant's efforts to keep them filled. The more you tense the harder you find it. Suddenly Jenny gets the message. The ski will float over the most alarming looking undulations which otherwise would throw her just to look at them. At the top she resists the temptation to let go too soon, waiting for the bar to slacken slightly on the run-out platform before gently letting it go (don't throw it, says her instructor) and easing out of the way of the next arrival. Tows, as she will soon find in the higher mountains, can sometimes go down as well as up. That is when you need your braking snowplough, which Jenny and Michael start to learn in the second phase of their instruction on day three.

The plough, or stem, is both a checking and a turning form for skis. Jenny, seeing the skis of learners in a V-shape, points almost together, could not understand why the points simply did not run into each other and turn the unfortunate skier head over heels. She tries it herself and sees that although the ski tips are pointing towards each other, her foot pressure keeps them going straight forward, but at a slower rate. If she digs in the inside edges equally on an easy slope she will come to a stop. The idea that she can stop by a technical device of her own making frees one big tension. Next Jenny is taught that sinking her weight on her right knee as she runs down the fall line will cause her to turn left, and vice versa for a right turn.

Quickly she is taught to link her turns, first one way and then another, then to bring her skis parallel for a short distance between turns. This speeds up the turns and eases her into the next phase, which is the basic swing, better known to older skiers as the stem christie turn, in which the inside ski is lifted or skidded alongside the outside ski in the fall line, and the swing is completed with skis parallel. Almost without realising it, Jenny learns to sideslip, flattening her skis to slip down a hill, edging them to stop herself, using the ski tails much more freely to dig in and check.

On day four, traversing, which is taking a descending diagonal line across a steeper slope, is interspersed with the other instruction. For this the skis are kept close together with weight mainly on the downhill ski and the uphill ski advanced about four inches.

Jenny learns to skid the tails of her skis downhill in a traverse, which checks speed, and notices how her upper body tends to react with shoulders and chest half-turning downhill. She at last understands the meaning of counter-rotation. By days five, six and eight of her fortnight, with a rest day in between, she is modestly competent with the basic swing. The natural, or hockey, stop has joined her repertoire almost without her noticing it. She is doing, in other words, what any youngster will do on a slide, turning the feet across the downhill line at right angles. If done at any speed it is quite a violent motion, knees down, up, then down again as she jumps her ski tails round her planted pole, skis finishing square to the slope and sliding a little downhill with the momentum. Only her legs have turned. Her head, arm and upper body keep facing downhill. This, she realises, is the basis of all advanced turns, although it short-cuts that dread arc through the fall line where the beginner so often loses his nerve, leans back on stiff legs, at once accelerates his skis and falls down backwards.

By day nine, in the second week, Jenny's group has suffered some changes. There is an element now of 'streaming' as the quicker learners, or those picking up the threads of earlier experience, are taken into the higher mountains to widen their knowledge and competence. New people have joined, others have stuck, possibly through a lack of fitness and natural athleticism, and need longer at the basics.

Jenny learns snowcraft as she goes along, but especially in days ten to twelve. She watches how people ahead are coping, following them where the going seems easy, picking a different path where they have obviously hit ice or bad ruts. She watches for fluffy snow where turning will be easier, and is taken to the side of mogul fields where bumps are less pronounced and the snow easier for slower turns or sideslipping. She learns how hard it is to traverse the bumps, which are shaped by better skiers going downwards rather than across. She is taught to ski on the downhill side of wood paths, which can be unnerving at the end of the day with their ice walls on the uphill side and rutted, icy centre sections. A slight stem is sometimes possible, but it is all too easy to catch an edge. There is more risk in running into a wall than semi-sideslipping on the outward side of the path, but the fear of a sudden catapult into the trees has to be overcome.

With experience, too, the ski codes take on meaning. On a T-bar you agree who skis off first, who 'takes the bar', which means letting it go gently, and not so that it flies around wildly, possibly endangering the skiers still clearing the platform. On the piste, the overtaking skier bears all the responsibility. He must do so safely. 'Achtung' in the German-speaking countries and 'Piste' in France are the shouts of warning. Jenny is advised always to stop on the side of a piste, never on a corner, in the centre of a narrow track, or over a brow. Moving off, always take a good look to ensure no-one is coming. After a fall, make sure you move out of the line of a faster skier's probable descent. Always study a map showing the grades of descent before tackling a strange mountain, and keep a sharp eye for the variously coloured runs. Outside the mountain restaurant, leave your skis where you can keep an eye on them, or in a carefully marked position. If you have lockable fitments in your hotel ski room, use them.

Coming out of her bindings in deep snow, Jenny is taught to form a cross with her sticks to lever herself up; then to compress the snow around to form a platform before putting her skis on again. Michael slightly sprains his thumb in a fall. At his hotel he asks for a simple plastic bag, fills it with snow, and wraps it round his thumb for half an hour. Ice bags should cost nothing in the Alps. After two more sessions like this to stop the internal bleeding, he is ready to apply hot water to restore healthy blood flow. Swelling is much reduced and his ski-ing is not too seriously bothered.

They are now fairly adept at the basic swing, which thousands of people find quite adequate for all the ski-ing they want, since it adapts to steep slopes and deep snow. However, a turn or swing with skis parallel from beginning to end is the natural goal for most younger, athletic skiers. All skiers must learn to absorb bumps and dips with legs giving and taking and the head kept in a level axis. In other words the legs are used as shock absorbers with the upper body reacting only as much as it needs to retain balance. Over-reaction by the upper body because of overtensed legs is the bane of the beginner and intermediate. With this partly overcome, Jenny discovers herself on day twelve turning with skis parallel. Up and down unweighting has occurred. She has switched ski leads at precisely the right moment. She has chosen exactly the right part of the slope to do it. She has kept most or all of her weight on the outside ski with the unweighted inside ski slightly forward. She will not be able to repeat it at will, but deep down in the unconscious something has clicked. She has proved herself to herself.

Jenny understands now that ski-ing poses an endless succession of summits: as one is conquered another looms. It is a recreation with a hard beginning, but with the right start, it should be harder still to stop. She finds pleasure, too, in the contrast between the physical effort and the comfort and warmth of the village. Ski life, she discovers, has a distinct pattern, the hours between 4 and 6.30 pm being among the most enjoyable, when people laugh and chat in the coffee shops, the konditorei and the crêperies, stroll around the shops, or take themselves off for a swim in the various hotel or public swimming baths. Après-ski can be dancing in the discotheque or, better, to a live group, with drinks a pound a time and sipped slowly. But Jenny equally enjoys the lingering bath, the drink in the stube before dinner, then the coffee and schnapps after a cosy, chatty meal. It is hard to be lonely in a ski village and, even if the sport had no other justification for her, Jenny would find it in this.

Appendix 1

Glossary of Ski-ing Terms

(F = French; G = German; I = Italian)

Abonnement (F). Season ticket for lifts or lessons.

Abfahrt (G). Downhill ski run (F: *Descente*), a test of speed and courage over two to three miles for men, and one to one and a half miles for women.

Achtung! (G). Danger! Look out! (F: *Piste!* I: *Pista!*).

Alm (G). Mountain pasture.

Alpine racing. Downhill, giant slalom and slalom races.

Ausgang (G). Out.

Avalement (F). Technique at the beginning and end of fast turns involving quick, flexible bending of the knees with feet thrust forward. Also Jet.

Bahnhof (G). Station.

Bindings. Devices which attach boot to ski.

Birdsnesting. Ski-ing off-piste among trees.

Bloodwagon. Sled for injured.

Cable car. Overhead suspension transport (G: *Luftseilbahn*; F: *Téléphérique*).

Chair lift. Overhead suspension transport, usually with double open seat (G: *Sesselbahn*; F: *Télésiège*; I: *Seggiovia*).

Christiania. Usually abbreviated to christie. Family of turns down and across the fall-line. In a parallel christie the skis are together, in a stem christie the outside ski fans out in a skidding style then returns to the parallel in traverse.

Counter-rotation. Angling of the upper body, so that the chest points down the slope when the legs are pointing across it.

Drag-lift. A system of cables by which skiers are pulled up a slope. Attachments are shaped into a 'T' for two people at a time, or a button, disc or 'soup plate' placed between the thighs for individuals.

Edging. Weighting the metal edges of skis to achieve check or turn.

Eingang (G). In.

Fall line. Steepest section below the skier at any given point.

Fermé (F). Closed (especially of a run with inadequate or dangerous snow conditions) (G: *Geschlossen, Gesperrt*).

FIS. Fédération Internationale de Ski, the world governing body of ski-ing.

Föhn (G). Warm wind producing thaw.

Funicular. Tracked railway for steep slopes.

Gaststube (G). Guest house (F: *Pension*).

Giant Slalom. One-mile race, especially testing traversing ability.

Glacier. Ice mass; summer ski-ing is often on glaciers.

GLM. Graduated length method. American teaching system in which pupils graduate from short ($1 \cdot 35$ metre) to longer lengths of ski as they progress (Also F: *Ski Evolutif*).

Gondola. Cabin cableway for two or four passengers. Known also as Bubbles (G: *Gondelbahn*; F: *Télécabines*).

Gunbarrel. Trail with upward-sloping sides, like a gutter.

Inside ski. Uphill ski (conversely outside ski = downhill ski).

Joch (G). Pass joining two peaks.

Kick turn. Changing direction through 180° from a stationary position.

Langlauf (G). *Langrenn* (N). Touring or cross-country ski-ing. Known also as *Ski de Fond* (F). Cross-country ski-ing and jumping are collectively known as Nordic, as opposed to Alpine, ski-ing.

Lehrer (G). Instructor. (F: *Moniteur*).

Loipe (N). Marked trail for Nordic skiers.

Moguls. Bumps made by the repeated passage of skiers.

Nursery slopes. Gentle gradients where beginners learn the rudiments of ski-ing.

Offen (G). *Ouvert* (F). Open: run open.

Parablacks. Plastic boxes fitted to the top of skis to help prevent them crossing in downhill racing or soft snow.

Piste (F). Marked track for Alpine skiers, implicitly with harder snow and more bumps because of the frequent passage of skiers.

Pole: Ski stick (G: *Stock*; F: *Baton*).

Pole plant. Use of the inside ski pole to initiate a turn, both timing it and helping with the up-unweighting.

Projection Circulaire (F). Turn of the body and skis with the outside arm leading.

P-Tex. Ski-sole material giving permanently waxy effect. Gouges can be repaired with a polythene candle.

Powder snow. New low-temperature snow.

Principianti (I). Beginners (G: *Anfänger*; F: *Débutantes*).

Safety strap. Strap attached to binding and clipping round the ankle to prevent the ski running away in a fall.

Schuss. Straight run down the fall-line without checks.

Sidestepping. Controlled sideways or diagonal slide, backwards or forwards.

Ski stoppers. U-shaped sprung clips with prongs attached to bindings which dig into the snow and stop a ski running away after a fall.

Slalom. Race of about 575 metres down a one-in-three slope through approximately 75 gates of beflagged poles not less then 3·20 metres apart. Test of turning ability.

Snow plough. Movement down or near the fall line with skis in a 'V' position, points together, ski soles turning to varying degrees, literally like a plough.

Snow plough turn. Change of direction made by weighting one or other of the skis when they are in the 'V' position.

Steilhang (G). Especially steep slope, always a feature of a classic downhill race.

Stem. Outward fanning movement of one or both skis, either to start a turn (see *Christiania*) or to take up the plough position.

Swing. Shallow turn.

Tramlines. Ruts.

Traverse. Movement across a slope, with slight to moderate drop.

Unfall (G). First aid post (F: *Poste de sécuritè*).

Verboten (G): Forbidden (F: *Defense de* . . .).

Wedel (G). Short, fast linked turns on flat or near flat skis down the fall line (F: *Godilles*).

Alpine Resorts

	Altitude (feet)		Lifts	Facilities*	Comments
	Village	Top station			
AUSTRIA					
Alpbach	3200	6600	15	X Cu P Sa	Charming Austrian village. Ski-ing all levels but especially beginners. Lively après-ski.
Badgastein	3600	9500	19	X Sk P Ca Sa	Well-known town resort and spa. Good uphill transport. Varied ski-ing. Varied night life.
Brand	3400	6200	8	X P Sa	Friendly family resort. All grades of ski-ing. Varied après-ski.
Ehrwald	3300	9700	6	X Sk Cu P	Charming village with attractive shops. Ski-ing good for beginners and intermediate. Lively après-ski.

Fieberbrunn	2600	5400	10	X Sk Sa	Spread out village. Good snow conditions. Ideal for young people. Energetic Tyrolean evenings.
Galtur	5200	7300	10	X Sk P Sa	Friendly informal village. Good for beginners and intermediates. A family resort.
Gargellen	4600	7100	7	P Sa	Small friendly resort. Ideal for families. Limited night life. Couple of advanced runs.
Gaschurn	3300	7300	10	P Sa	Centre of excellent new ski complex. Suitable for the intermediate skier. Lively night life.
Gerlos	4100	6800	12	X P	Attractive village. Suitable for families. Good kindergarten with ski-ing. Beginners to intermediate ski-ing.
Hinterglemm	3600	6900	19	X Cu P Sa	Suitable for beginners and intermediates. Connected to nearby Saalbach. More informal. Friendly atmosphere.
Hintertux	4900	10700	10	X Sk Cu P Ca	Very high resort, above Mayrhofen. Intermediate to expert standard. Some beginners' runs. Quiet night life.

* X – Cross-country, Sk – Skating, Cu – Curling, P – Pool, Ca – Casino, Sa – Sauna, H – Hospital

	Altitude (feet) Village	Top station	Lifts	Facilities*	Comments
Igls	3000	7400	6	Sk P	Close to Innsbruck so suitable for all-round holiday. Beginners to intermediate skiers mainly. Good night life.
Ischgl	4600	9800	15	X Sk P Sa	Informal and charming with ski-ing for all grades, but mainly beginners to intermediate. Good après-ski.
Kaprun	2600	10000	14	X P	Excellent area for summer ski-ing especially. Varied night life. Close to good ski-ing at Zell-am-Zee.
Kirchberg	2800	6500	15	X Sk Cu P Sa	Attractive Tyrolean village close to Kitzbühel. Extensive ski-ing. Good night life.
Kitzbühel	2600	6600	52	X Sk Cu P Ca Sa H	Wide choice of ski-ing on mainly intermediate runs. Sophisticated, expensive, attractive international town.
Lech	4700	7800	27	X Sk Cu P Sa	A top resort. Unlimited ski-ing for all standards. Internationally known, chic but very charming. Good night life.

Lermoos	3300	7000	6	X Sk P Sa	Picturesque unsophisticated Tyrolean village. All grades of ski-ing. Good nursery slopes. Lots of après-ski.
Leutasch	3700	5300	9	X Sk Cu P Sa	Friendly unsophisticated village. Suitable for beginners but close to amenities of Seefeld.
Lienz	2400	7500	10	X Sk Cu P Sa H	Small compact town, attractive and friendly. Beginners to intermediate ski-ing. Suitable for families. Good après-ski.
Mallnitz	4000	8800	10	X Sk P Ca Sa	Suitable for families. Beginners to intermediate ski-ing. Quiet resort but possibilities for fun.
Mayrhofen	2100	6600	15	X Sk Cu P Sa	Large village of great charm. Lively après-ski. Ski-ing for all grades. Something for everyone.
Niederau	3100	5000	10	X Sk	Three villages about two miles apart. (Niederau, Oberau, Auffach). Good for beginners.
Ober/Hochgurgl	6300	10100	18	X P Sa	Highest resorts in Austria – very good snow record. Beginners to experts. Families. Varied night life.

* X – Cross-country, Sk – Skating, Cu – Curling, P – Pool, Ca – Casino, Sa – Sauna, H – Hospital

| | Altitude (feet) | | Lifts | Facilities* | Comments |
	Village	Top station			
Pertisau	3100	5000	6	X Sk Cu P Sa	Attractive lakeside village, north facing slopes, good snow conditions. Intermediate ski-ing.
St Anton	4300	9300	26	X Sk Cu P Sa H	Top cosmopolitan resort. Fantastic ski-ing above beginner standard. Chic expensive night life.
St Johann	2200	5300	8	X Sk P Sa H	Attractive town resort close to Kitzbühel. Extensive ski terrain.
Saalbach	3300	6800	43	X Sk Cu P Sa	Good ski-ing all grades, mainly beginners and intermediates. Semi-sophisticated village. Varied night life.
Schruns	2300	7600	7	X Sk P Sa H	Small attractive town resort. Limited ski-ing for all grades. Centre of the excellent Montafon complex.
Seefeld	4000	7000	16	X Sk Cu P Ca Sa	Lively resort close to Innsbruck, good facilities. Ski-ing beginners to intermediate. Varied après-ski.
Serfaus	4700	7900	12	X Sk Cu P Ca Sa	Sunny relaxed mountain village, mainly for beginners and intermediate skiers. Lively night life.

Solden (inc. Hochs)	4600	10000	22	X Sk Cu P Sa	Between Solden and nearby Hochsolden, there is ski-ing for all grades. Good après-ski and shops.
Soll	2300	6000	16	X Sk Cu P Sa	Attractive village. Interesting ski-ing, mainly for the less experienced. Good night life.
Steinach	3500	6600	6	X Sk Cu P Sa	Village on Brenner Pass, mainly for beginners.
Westendorf	2600	6000	10	Sk	Friendly sunny village in the Kitzbühel Alps. Excellent for learning. Lively night life.
Zell-am-Zee	2500	6500	20	X Sk Cu P Sa H	Ski town with good runs to expert grade. More ski-ing at nearby Saalbach and Kaprun. Informal night life.
Zurs	5700	8700	10	P Sa H	Small village on road to Lech. Excellent Arlberg ski-ing. Close to Lech night life.
FRANCE
Alpe d'Huez	6100	11000	38	X Sk Cu P Sa	Chic, fairly expensive resort with great sunny area with lots of ski-ing for all grades. Good après-ski.

* X – Cross-country, Sk – Skating, Cu – Curling, P – Pool, Ca – Casino, Sa – Sauna, H – Hospital

| | Altitude (feet) | | Lifts | Facilities* | Comments |
	Village	Top station			
Avoriaz	5900	7400	16	Sk P Sa	Very modern traffic-free resort. Ski-ing for all grades.
Chamonix	3400	12500	33	Sk Cu P Ca Sa H	Town resort with fantastic ski-ing. Varied night life. Lots going on.
Chamrousse	5400	7400	22	X Sk Cu P Ca	Two or three modern, spaced out centres close to Grenoble. Good ski-ing all grades. Good lift system.
Courchevel	3900	8200	55	X Sk Cu P Sa	First of the French ski stations designed for skiers. A top resort. Modern, chic. Fantastic ski-ing.
Flaine	5200	8200	25	X Sk P Sa	Very modern, good resort for ski fanatic. No traffic. Good resort for young. Children well catered for.
Isola 2000	6600	8100	13	X Sk P Sa H	Modern station close to Nice. All buildings interconnected. Good ski-ing all grades.
La Clusaz	3600	7800	32	X Sk P Sa	Long established and charming chalet resort. Good ski-ing all grades. Lively après-ski.

La Plagne	6500	8100	50	X P Sa H	Modern, custom-built for skiers. Wide open ski-ing for intermediate skiers. Average night life.
Le Corbier	5100	7500	13	X Sk Cu P Sa	Very new, custom-built. Very reliable snow conditions. Ski-ing all grades.
Les Arcs	5400	9900	33	X P Sa	Modern, custom-built station. Good ski-ing all grades. Chic atmosphere.
Les Carroz	3500	5600	8	X Sk Sa	Small Alpine-type village. Good for families, beginners and intermediate skiers.
Les Deux Alpes	5500	12000	50	X Sk P Sa	Rather spaced out resort with lots of young French. Sunny slopes. Ski-ing all grades. Not chic.
Les Menuires	5500	10200	25	P Sa	Very modern. Ski-ing interconnects with Meribel-Courchevel. All grades.
Luchon	2100	7200	12	P Sa	Town resort with nearby ski-ing. Good for all-round holiday. Great character.
Megève	3700	6700	31	X Sk Cu P Ca Sa	Old village, great charm. Chic, expensive. Good night life. Medium ski-ing. Good off-piste.

* X – Cross-country, Sk – Skating, Cu – Curling, P – Pool, Ca – Casino, Sa – Sauna, H – Hospital

| | Altitude (feet) | | | | |
	Village	Top station	Lifts	Facilities*	Comments
Méribel	4800	8900	29	X Sk P Sa	Extensive ski area linked with Courchevel and Les Menuires. Very charming. All grade ski-ing.
Montgenèvre	6100	8900	38	X Sk Cu H	Best for beginners and intermediate family skiers. Attractive, unsophisticated resort.
Pra-Loup	5400	8300	22	X Sk P Sa	Modern, well laid out resort connected with La Foux d'Allos. Varied ski-ing.
St Gervais	2600	5800	22	X Sk Cu P Ca Sa	Friendly family resort. Access to Chamonix and Megève ski-ing.
St Lary	2600	7900	20	X P Sa	Best for families, beginners and intermediates. Pleasant atmosphere.
Serre Chevalier	4400	8200	44	X Sk P Sa	Central village within group. Wide open slopes. Ski-ing all grades.
Superdevoluy	4900	8200	15	X P Sa	Good ski-ing for intermediates and beginners. Shops, restaurants, all in one building.
Tignes	6900	9900	57	X Sk Cu P Sa	Large modern ski area. All grades. Chic night life.

Val d'Isère	6000	10700	57	X Sk Cu P Sa	International resort, great variety of runs, connected with Tignes. Intermediates to advanced will best appreciate it. Reliable snow.
Val Thorens	7600	10900	19	X P Sa	Modern resort, connected with Courchevel and Méribel. Open ski-ing.
ITALY Bormio	4000	10000	16	X Sk P Sa	Very old spa resort. Ski-ing all grades. Attractive shops and bars. Lively night life. Summer ski-ing near.
Cervinia	6700	11500	15	X Sk P Sa	Fun-loving resort. Ski-ing all grades. Summer ski-ing. Excellent spring snow.
Chiesa	3200	7000	6	Sk	Typical Italian mountain village. Ski-ing suitable beginners and intermediate. Unsophisticated night life.
Cortina	4000	10700	41	Sk P Sa	International resort with varied ski-ing and après-ski. Sophisticated but expensive.
Corvara	5100	7800	33	X Sk Cu P Sa	Small Dolomite village. Best for beginners and intermediates. Connected to other villages. Fun night life.

*X – Cross-country, Sk – Skating, Cu – Curling, P – Pool, Ca – Casino, Sa – Sauna, H – Hospital

	Altitude (feet)				
	Village	Top station	Lifts	Facilities*	Comments
Courmayeur	4000	11400	27	Sk P	Small spread-out town resort with character. Reasonable ski-ing all grades. Good night life. Summer ski-ing.
Livigno	6000	9600	23	Sk P Sa	Duty-free 'skiers' resort. Ski-ing all grades. Spread-out village, not much character. Good night life.
Macugnaga	4400	9500	15	Sk Cu P Sa	Consists of two small villages. Good nursery slopes and average and upwards grades. Informal après-ski.
Madesimo	5100	8900	14	X Sk Cu P Sa	Excellent nursery slopes. Ski-ing all grades. Small, friendly, unsophisticated resort.
Madonna di C.	5000	8200	20	X Sk Cu Ca Sa	One of Italy's leading resorts. Lots of ski-ing all grades. Quite modern, chic and sophisticated.
Ortisei	4100	8100	28	X Sk Cu Sa	Small town with character. Massive ski area but gentle slopes more suitable for beginners to medium.
Sauze d'Oulx	5000	8100	12	X Sk	Small friendly village with good ski-ing for beginners to intermediates.

Sestrière	6700	8800	25	X Sk P Sa	International resort of renown. Not very attractive, but lots going on. Ski-ing all grades.
Solda	6300	8900	12	P	Small spread-out resort. Limited but interesting ski-ing. Not much night life but very friendly.
La Thuile	4700	8600	8	X H	Lovely village resort in the Aosta valley. Interesting ski-ing and close to Mont Blanc.
Vason M. Bondone	3300	6900	9	X Sk Cu	Three connected villages. Beautiful scenery. Interesting ski-ing, but not for the expert.
SWITZERLAND Adelboden	4600	7700	25	X Sk Cu P Sa	Friendly, happy resort. Some expert ski-ing. Mainly for beginners to intermediate. Wide variety night life.
Andermatt	4800	9800	9	X Sk Cu Sa H	High and sometimes very cold. Some of the best snow in the Alps. Ski-ing all grades. Unsophisticated après-ski.

*X – Cross-country, Sk – Skating, Cu – Curling, P – Pool, Ca – Casino, Sa – Sauna, H – Hospital

| | Altitude (feet) | | | | |
	Village	Top station	Lifts	Facilities*	Comments
Anzere	5000	7900	9	X Sk Cu P Sa	Small modern custom-built village. No cars. Good for families. On sunny plateau.
Arosa	5600	8700	10	X Sk Cu P Ca Sa H	Large chic sophisticated resort. Ski-ing all grades. Lots for non-skier. Lots of night life.
Chateau d'Oex	3300	5800	11	X Sk Cu P Sa	Small charming village near Gstaad.
Crans-Montana	5000	9900	32	X Sk Cu P Ca Sa H	Wide open area with good ski-ing for beginners and intermediates upwards. Varied night life.
Davos	5100	8300	37	X Sk Cu P Ca Sa H	Town resort with huge sprawling ski areas, notably the Parsenn. Diverse night life. Sophisticated, not cheap.
Engelberg	3400	9900	18	X Sk Cu P Ca Sa H	Picturesque village. Atmosphere and good ski-ing all grades. Plenty of après-ski.
Flims	3600	9200	25	X Sk Cu P Sa	Spread-out resort. Good all-grade ski-ing. Plenty of comfortable hotels.
Grindelwald	3500	11400	23	X Sk Cu P Sa	Good all-grade ski-ing. Connected with Wengen. Spectacular scenery beneath Eiger. Adequate night life.

Gstaad	3600	9800	16	X Sk Cu P Ca Sa H	Smart resort. Gentle ski-ing. Beautiful village.
Klosters	4000	9900	24	X Sk Cu P Sa	International resort. Excellent ski-ing linked with Davos. Chic but expensive night life.
Lenzerheide	4900	9400	31	X Sk Cu P Sa	Relaxed, sprawling, well-treed resort. All grade ski-ing, but particularly up to medium grade. Not chic.
Leysin	4100	7300	13	X Sk Cu P Sa	Ski-ing good up to medium standard. Beautiful setting.
Malbun	5300	6600	7	X Sk P Sa	Liechtenstein village. Sunny, good ski-ing to third year.
Mürren	5400	10000	11	X Sk Cu Sa	Spectacular setting, challenging runs. A 'British' resort. Home of Kandahar Ski Club. Comfortable hotels.
Pontresina	6000	10500	17	X Sk Cu P	Good ski-ing, particularly on Diavolezza. Not so expensive as nearby St Moritz. Substantial hotels.
Saas-Fée	6100	9900	20	X Sk Cu P Sa	Village resort, favourite of English and Germans. Good compact ski-ing, excellent ski school.

*X – Cross-country, Sk – Skating, Cu – Curling, P – Pool, Ca – Casino, Sa – Sauna, H – Hospital

| | Altitude (feet) | | | | |
	Village	Top station	Lifts	Facilities*	Comments
St Moritz	6100	10900	48	X Sk Cu P Ca Sa H	International resort. Exceptional ski-ing and night life. Expensive. Cresta tobogganing, bobsleigh, curling, etc. Voyeur's delight.
Verbier	5000	10000	30	X Sk Cu P Sa H	Chalet resort. International clientele. Excellent ski-ing. Limited après-ski. Expensive.
Villars	4300	7300	28	X Sk Cu P Sa	Small, attractive old-established resort. Comfortable hotels. Good ski-ing to intermediate.
Wengen	4300	11400	17	Sk Cu P Ca Sa	Old-established resort, long popular with traditional English. Ski-ing all grades. Sunny. Home of Downhill Only club.
Zermatt	5300	11600	25	X Sk Cu P Sa	Truly 'big' ski-ing, though not much for beginners. Carless, picturesque village. Chic but expensive.

Appendix 3

Artificial Ski Slopes in Great Britain

Aberdeenshire
Aberdeen: Kaimhill Ski Slope, Earthdee Road. Telephone: 23456

Angus
Dundee: Ancrum Activities Centre, 10 Ancrum Road. 60719

Ayrshire
Kilmarnock: Newmilns Ski Slope. 25628

Berkshire
Reading: Bulmershe Ski Slope, Bulmershe College of Higher Education, Woodlands Avenue, Woodley. 67387
Carter & Son Ltd, 99 Caversham Road. 55589

Avon
Bristol: Bryant Outdoor Centre, Colston Street. 23166

Caenarvon
Betwys-Y-Coed: Plas-Y-Brenin National Mountaineering Centre, Capel Curig. Capel Curig 214

Cheshire
Bebington: Oval Sports Centre. 051 645 3020
Runcorn: Squash Ski Runcorn, Palace Fields. 64104
Stalybridge: Indoor Sports, Castle Street. 061 338 3528

Westvale: Kirkby Ski Slope, Kirkby Stadium, Whitefield Drive. 051 546 3104

Co. Antrim
Lisburn: Castle Robin Ski Slope. 669519

Co. Armagh
Craigavon: Craigavon Golf & Ski Centre, Silverwood, Lurgan. Lurgan 6606

Co. Durham
Sunderland: Seaburn Ocean Park Ski Slope.

Cumbria
Carlisle: Carlisle & District Ski Club, Edenside. Wetheral 60244
Workington: West Cumberland Ski Club, Ehenside School, Cleator Moor. 4906

Devon
Exeter: Exeter & District Ski Club, Clifton Hill Sports Centre. 74303
Torquay: Wessex Ski Association, Lydwell Road. 080 264 127

Essex
Basildon: Aquatels Recreation Centre.
Brentwood: Warley Ski School, Warley Sports Centre, Holdens Wood, Warley Gap. 211994
Harlow: Harlow Ski Centre, Harlow Sports Centre, Hamarskjold Road. 26313

Fife
Glenrothes: Fife Institute of Physical & Recreational Education, Viewfield Road. 771700

Flint
Deeside: North-East Wales Institute, Kelsterton College, Connah's Quay. 817531 ext. 269

Glamorgan
Cardiff: Cardiff Ski Centre, Fairwater. 0222 561 793

Gloucestershire
Gloucester: Gloucester Ski Centre, Matson Lane. 414300

Hampshire
Aldershot: Stainforth Ski School, Hurst Road. 24431 ext. 2299
Eastleigh: Eastleigh Sports Centre, Passfield Avenue. 7416
Southampton: Southampton Ski Slope, The Sports Centre, Bassett. 68598
Calshot Activities Centre, Calshot Spit. Fawley 892077

Hertfordshire
Royston: Bassingbourne Barracks. 42271 ext. 212
Watford: Watford Ski School, Woodside Playing Fields, Horseshoe Lane, Garston. Garston (Herts) 76550
Welwyn Garden City: Welwyn Garden City Ski Centre, Gosling Stadium, Stanborough Road. 29025

Inverness-shire
Aviemore: Drambuie Ski Slope, Aviemore Centre. 296

Kent
Folkestone: Folkestone Sports Centre, Radnor Park Avenue. 58222
Tunbridge Wells: Bowles Outdoor Pursuits Centre, Eridge. Crowborough 4127

Lanarkshire
Glasgow: Bearsden Ski Club, The Mound, Stockiemuir Road, Courthill, Bearsden. 041 942 2933
Bellahouston, 16 Dumbreck. 041 427 0558

Lancashire
Lancaster: Physical Education Dept, Lancaster & Morecambe College of Further Education, Morecambe Road. 66215

Manchester: Manchester Ski School, Ellis Brigham, 6–14 Cathedral Street. 061 834 0161

Newchurch in Pendle: Pendle Ski Club, Old School House. Nelson 62633

Oldham: Ski Counthill, c/o Amenities & Recreation Dept, Alexandra Park. 061 624 8286

Rossendale: Ski Rossendale, Oakenhead Wood, Haslingden Old Road, Rawtenstall. 28844

London: Alexandra Palace Ski Centre, Alexandra Park, N22. 01 888 2284
Crystal Palace National Sports Centre, Norwood, SE19. 01 778 0131
Woolwich Garrison, Greenhill Terrace, SE18.

Middlesex
Uxbridge: Hillingdon Ski Centre, Park Road. 55183

Midlothian
Edinburgh: Hillend Ski Centre, Biggar Road. 031 445 4433

Monmouthshire
Pontypool: The Sports Centre. 56955

Norfolk
Norwich: Norfolk Ski Slope, Whittingham Lane, Trowse. Walcott 442

Northamptonshire
Rushden: Skew Bridge Ski Club, Northampton Road. 3808

Northumberland
Morpeth: Northumberland Ski Slope, Cottingwood Lane. Gosforth 850181

Nottinghamshire
Nottingham: Carlton Forum Ski School, Foxhill Road, Carlton. 871434

Oxfordshire
Brize Norton: Brize Norton Ski Centre, RAF Brize Norton.
  099 384 2551

Shropshire
Telford: Telford Ski Slope, Court Centre, Court Street,
  Madeley. 586791

Somerset
Wellington: Wellington Sports Centre, Corams Lane. 3010

Staffordshire
Kidsgrove: Kidsgrove Ski Centre, Bathpool Park. 5342
Wednesbury: Tebbutt's Ski School, 35 Market Place. 021 556
  0802

Stirlingshire
Polmont: Polmonthill Ski Centre, Polmont Farm. 3660

Surrey
Esher: Sandown Ski Schools Ltd, Sandown Park, More Lane.
  65588
Guildford: Guildford Church of England Secondary School,
  Larch Avenue. 4324

Sussex
Brighton: Sports & Leisure Ski School, 47/48 North Street.
  29539

Warwickshire
Birmingham: Hard's Birmingham Ski School, Cricket Ground,
  Edgbaston. 021 643 8549
  Birmingham Ski School, The Mountain Shop, 18/19 Snow
  Hill, Queensway. 021 236 6816

Worcestershire
Dudley: Dudley Ski Centre, c/o Dudley Zoo, 2 The Broadway.
  58648

Yorkshire

Catterick: Catterick Ski Slope, Loos Road, Catterick Garrison.
    Catterick Camp 3788

Harrogate: Harrogate Ski Centre, Great Yorkshire Showground,
    Hookstone Wood Road.

Leeds: Centresport Ski School, Centresport (Leeds) Ltd, 40
    Woodhouse Lane. 42079

Appendix 4

Useful Addresses

Andorra, 63 Westover Road, London SW18. 874 4806

Austrian National Tourist Office, 30 St George Street, London W1. 629 0461

Aviemore Information Centre, Aviemore, Inverness-shire. 363

Finnish Tourist Board, 56 Haymarket, London SW1. 839 4048

French Government Tourist Office, 179 Piccadilly, London W1. 493 3171

German National Tourist Office, 61 Conduit Street, London W1. 734 2600

Italian State Tourist Dept (ENIT), 201 Regent Street, London W1. 439 2311

Norwegian National Tourist Office, 20 Pall Mall, London SW1. 839 6255

Polish Tourist Centre, 313 Regent Street, London W1. 580 8028

Scottish Tourist Board, 137 Knightsbridge, Lonson SW1. 589 2218

Spanish National Tourist Board, 70 Jermyn Street, London SW1. 930 8578

Spey Valley – Ness Travel, 32 Academy Street, Inverness. 39481

Swiss National Tourist Office, Swiss Centre, 1 New Coventry Street, London W1. 734 1921

TOUR OPERATORS

Blue Sky Holidays, London Road, East Grinstead, Sussex. East Grinstead 28211

CIT, 10 Charles II Street, London SW1. 686 5533

Crawford Perry, 260A Fulham Road, London SW10. 351 2191

Erna Low/Enjoy Britain & the World Travel Service, 21 Old Brompton Road, London SW7. 584 9010

Global, 200 Tottenham Court Road, London W1. 637 3333

Hards Travel Service, 1A Corporation Street, Birmingham 15. 021 643 7962

Horizon, 214 Broad Street, Birmingham 15. 021 632 6222

Inghams, 329 Putney Bridge Road, London SW15. 789 6555

James Vance Travel, 421 Edgware Road, London NW9. 205 4006

John Morgan Travel, 30 Thurloe Place, London SW7. 589 5478

Montpelier Travel, 17 Montpelier Street, London SW7. 589 8206

Small World, 5 Garrick Street, London WC2. 240 3233

Stephen Lord Holidays, 29 Queen Square, Bristol. Bristol 297726

Supertravel, 21/22 Hans Place, London SW1. 589 5161

Swans, 2 The Causeway, Bishop's Stortford, Herts. Bishop's Stortford 55911

Swiss Chalets, 10 Sheen Road, Richmond, Surrey. 948 4112

Swiss Travel, Bridge House, Ware, Herts. Ware 61221

Thomsons, Greater London House, Hampstead Road, London NW1. 388 0681

Waymark Holidays, 295 Lillie Road, London SW6. 385 5015

SKI CLUBS

England and Northern Ireland

Clubs may be contacted through the Regional Ski Associations as follows.

London and South-East: Denis Nelson, 5 Coombe Road, Yateley, Nr. Camberley, Surrey. (London, Surrey, Sussex, Kent)

Southern: Derek Abbott, TAAB Laboratories, 52 Kidmore End Road, Emmer Green, Reading. (Berks, Bucks, Hants, Oxford.)

South-West: Mrs Jill Pearson, Rowlands, Shute, Axminster, Devon. (Devon, Somerset, Dorset, Cornwall.)

Eastern: Ivan Palfrey, Solar Via, Happisburgh, Norwich. (Beds, Hunts, Suffolk, Norfolk, Essex, Cambs, Herts.)

West Midland: Stan Palmer, 9 Reeves Gardens, Codsall, Staffs. (Shropshire, Stafford, Hereford, Worcester, Warwick.)

East Midland: Dr Elder-Smith, Tristans, Grandfield Crescent, Radcliffe-on-Trent, Nottingham. (Derby, Nottingham, Lincoln less Lindsay, Leicester, Rutland, Northampton.)

North-West: Derek Lunt, 20 Aldwych Road, Liverpool 12. (Lancs, Cheshire, Peak District.)

North-East: Bill Hall, 3 Valley Close, Tow Law, Co. Durham. (Northumberland, Durham, Yorks NR.)

Yorkshire and Humberside: Ivor Davies, 50 Turnsteads Avenue, Cleckheaton, Yorkshire. (Yorks ER, Yorks WR, Lindsay.)

Ulster Ski Federation: Ian McIntyre, Plycol Montgomerie (NI Ltd) Falcon Road, Belfast, BT9 6RB. (Northern Ireland.)

Scotland and Wales

Clubs may be contacted through the national Ski Councils, as follows.

Scotland: Scottish National Ski Council, The Barn, Balmore, Torrance, Glasgow.

Wales: Ski Council for Wales, c/o Mrs Belinda Fairfax-Luxmoore, Castell Howell, Llandyssul, Dyfed.

SKI SHOPS

Aberdeenshire
Aberdeen: Marshalls, 302 George Street.
   Campbell's Sports, 520 Union Street.

Angus
Dundee: David Low Sports, 21 Commercial Street.
   Lillywhites, Draffens, Nethergate.

Avon
Bristol: Bryant Outdoor Centre, Colston Street.
   Ellis Brigham, 162 Whiteladies Road.
   Pindisports, 5 Welsh Back.
   Tratman & Lowther Ltd., Berkeley Place.

Ayrshire
Ayr: Ian Luke Sports, 42 Carrick Street.

Bedfordshire
Bedford: Jeans (of Bedford), 40 Allhallows.

Berkshire
Reading: Carters Ski Centre, 99 Caversham Road.

Buckinghamshire
Gerrards Cross: Woodward & Stalder.
High Wycombe: Woodward & Stalder, Thame House.

Caernarvonshire
Capel Curig: Ellis Brigham.

Cambridgeshire
Cambridge: The Cambridge Out-door Centre, 7 Bridge Street.

Cheshire
Stockport: Base Camp, 89 Lower Hillgate.

Co. Durham
Sunderland: Reynolds Outdoor Centre, 6 Derwent Street.

Cumberland
Carlisle: Sporthaus, 2 The Crescent.
Keswick: Geo. Fisher, 2 Borrowdale Road.

Derbyshire
Derby: Prestige, 350 Normanton Street.

Devon
Exeter: Grays of Exeter, 181/182 Sidwell Street.
 J. Webber Sports, 79 Queens Street.
 Wessex Sports, South Street.
Torquay: Tuckerman's Sports, 6/7 Victoria Parade, The
 Harbour.

Dorset
Poole: Calypso Sports, 18 Bournemouth Road, Parkstone.

Dunbartonshire
Dumbarton: Ian Tyrell Sports, 20 High Street.

Glamorgan
Cardiff: Cardiff Sportsgear, 81 Whitechurch Road.

Gloucestershire
Cheltenham: Horace Barton, 12 Regent Street.

Hampshire
Southampton: Snow Togs, 429/431 Millbrook Road.

Hertfordshire
Hemel Hempstead: Don Farrell Ltd, 254 Marlowes.
St Albans: Jeans (St Albans) Ltd, 14 Victoria Street.

Inverness-shire
Aviemore: D'Ecosse Ski & Sports Ltd.
   Aviemore Centre.
   Cairdsport.
   Speyside Sports.
   David Low, Scottish Norwegian Ski School, Cairngorm
      Hotel.
Kingussie: Badenoch Sports, High Street.

Kent
Tunbridge Wells: Leisure Life, 12 Union Square, The Pantiles.

Lanarkshire
East Kilbride: Ian Luke Sports, 6 Brouster Gate.
Glasgow: Blacks of Greenock, 132 Vincent Street.
   Cairdsport, Duncan Yacht Chandlers, 49 W. Nile Street.
   Greaves Sports, 23 Gordon Street.
   Ian Luke Sports, 170 Battlefield Road.
   Ian Luke Sports, 247 Kilmarnock Road, Shawlands.

Lancashire
Blackburn: Mountain Craft, 18 Darwen Street.
Blackpool: The Alpine Centre, 193/5 Church Street.
Bolton: Alpine Sports, 117 Bradshawgate.
Lancaster: H. Robinson, 5 New Road.
Liverpool: Ellis Brigham, 73 Bold Street.
   Don Morrison, 43 Harrington Street, L2.
Manchester: Ellis Brigham, 12/14 Cathedral Street.
   Stubbs Outdoor Sports, 211 Deansgate.
   YHA, 36/38 Fountain Street.

Preston: Preston Sports Depot, 141 Friargate.
Broughton in Furness: Mountain Centre, Brad Street and
   Market Street.

Leicestershire
Leicester: Redmayne & Todd, London Road.
   R. Turner, 105 London Road.

London
  Alpine Sports, 309 Brompton Road, SW3.
  Alpine Sports, 10/12 Holborn, EC1.
  Don Farrell Ltd, 14 Holmstall Parade, Burnt Oak, Edgware.
  Harrods Ltd, Knightsbridge, SW1.
  Lillywhites Ltd, Piccadilly Circus, SW1.
  Gordon Lowes Ltd, 173/174 Sloane Street, SW1.
  Lucas Sports Ltd, Unit C, 10 Brent Cross, NW4.
  Lucas Sports Ltd, 1 New College Parade, Finchley Road,
    Swiss Cottage, NW3.
  Lucas Sports Ltd, 1/3 Mercer Walk, New Town Centre,
    Uxbridge.
  Lucas Sports Ltd, 81 Wigmore Street, W1.
  Lucas Sports Ltd, 84 Victoria Street, SW1.
  Lucas Sports Ltd, 58 Riverdale New Town Centre,
    Lewisham.
  Bill Kent, 19 Aylmer Parade, Gt. North Road, N2.
  Moss Bros Ltd, Bedford Street, Covent Garden, WC2.
  Pindisports, 13/17 Brompton Arcade, SW3.
  Pindisports, 14 Holborn, EC1.
  Pindisports, 26 Old Bond Street, W1.
  Simpsons, Piccadilly, SW1.
  The Ski Shop, 158 Notting Hill Gate, W11.
  Sun & Snow, 18 Bute Street, SW7.
  Weinsteins of Lewisham, Lee High Road, SE13.
  YHA Services, 29 John Adam Street, WC2.

Midlothian
Edinburgh: Skisport & Sun, Barclay Terrace.
  R. W. Forsyth, Princes Street.
  Hans Sports, 139 Commiston Road.
  Lillywhites, 129 Princes Street.
  Ian Luke Sports, 28 Howe Street.

Morayshire
Grantown: Speyside Sports.

Norfolk
Norwich: Pilch, 1 Brigg Street.

Northumberland
Newcastle-on-Tyne: Montane Ltd, 12 Grey Street.

Nottinghamshire
Nottingham: R. Turner, Mountain Sports, 120 Derby Road.
  Redmayne & Todd, Carrington Street.
  Surfside & Alpine Sports, 11 Old Brickyard, Honeywood
    Gardens.

Oxfordshire
Oxford: Elmer Cotton Ltd, Prama House, Summertown.

Perthshire
Glenshee: Cairdsport, Spittal of Glenshee.
  Cairnwell Sports, Glenshee Chairlift.
Perth: Banks of Perth, 29 St. John Street.

Renfrewshire
Greenock: Ian Luke Sports, 124 Cathcart Street.

Staffordshire
Wednesbury: Tebbutts, 35 Market Place.
Wolverhampton: Wulfrum Camp, King Street.

Stirlingshire
Bridge of Allan: McLarens, 4 Ailen Vale Road.
Stirling: Alexander Sports Centre, Friar Street.

Surrey
Croydon: Pindisports, 1098 Whitgift Centre.
Esher: Europa Ski Lodge, Moor Lane.
Farnham: Supa Sports, East Street.
Guildford: Supa Sports, 160 High Street.
Walton: Supa Sports, 25 High Street.
Woking: Supa Sports, Church Path.

Sussex
Horsham: Tony Smith Sports, 35/37 East Street and 2 Park
  Street.

Chichester: Russell Hillsdon Ltd, 46 South Street.
   Chichester Ski School, Goodwood Race Course.
Brighton: Sport & Leisure, 47/48 North Street
   Alpine Sports, 138 Western Road.

Warwickshire
Birmingham: The Mountain Shop, 18/19 Snowhill, Queensway.
   Pindisports, 27/29 Martineau Square.
   Oswald Bailey, 114 Newtown Shopping Centre.
   YHA, 35 Cannon Street.

Westmorland
Ambleside: The Climbers Shop, Compston Corner.

Yorkshire
Bradford: Brown, Muff's, 26 Market Street.
Halifax: The Outdoor Centre, 3 Princess Arcade.
Harrogate: The Sports Depot Ltd, 47 Parliament Street.
Leeds: Centresport, Merrion Centre.
   Lillywhites, Trinity Street Arcade.
Middlesbrough: Cleveland Mountain Sports, 98 Newport Road.
Sheffield: B. Stokes, 9 Charles Street.
Skipton: Dales Outdoor Centre, Coach Street.
York: W. Hargreaves & Son, 85 Walmgate.

Index